MW00917500

Blue Jean Theology:
Basic Doctrine for Every Day Christians

By Matthew Sherro

ISBN: 9781520233178

In Loving Memory
Marie Tank (Mom) 12/07/1956 - 01/04/2012
Cynthia McLean (Grandmother) 05/06/1925-06/20/1995

For my favorite Students
Donna Riza M. Sherro

Lauro B Trejo III
Luis Hernandez

Dedicatory
Most importantly, this work is offered for Christ and His glory. He is both our Redeemer and Reward and we long for His coming.

Special Thanks to:
Wayne Kinde
Doug Warwick
Dr. Gary Coombs
Mike Turany

Introduction

Doctrine: It can be a scary word. It implies not only that you believe something, but that you can also explain that belief and defend it. It is also a very important word as it is doctrine that defines the Church. Jude referenced what he called our common salvation as the intent of his letter and what he meant there was doctrine. I will address the definition of doctrine in a moment, but before we do that, I want to address two questions that I have been asked, a couple dozen times, about this project.

Why do we need yet another systematic theology textbook and why are you teaching theology?First, this is not a systematic theology textbook. Systematic Theology covers many more topics than we will cover here; this is simply a self-study guide for new Christians and/or people who have never really studied their doctrine before. Secondly, theology is simply the study of God and since it is very hard to have a relationship with someone that you do not know, a basic understanding of certain Foundational Principles is required.

While I will, at times, lean toward the academic, we will try to take a pastoral approach throughout this text. The pastor must be a theologian and must guard the faith for his congregation; at the same time, he must give them their spiritual food and that food must be in a format that can be processed by the congregation. That, then, is why we have this book when there are so many other good texts out there; most are very academic (which is not per se bad) and I wanted to offer something additional so that those who do not enjoy an academic style text can benefit as well.

Note: The Study Notes, here, are an adaptation of my notes from my Foundations Series at http://exploringthetruth.org This is not intended to be a traditional text on doctrine. Instead, these notes are meant to guide your self study into the doctrinal basis of our faith.

So what is doctrine? Dictionary.com defines doctrine as a particular principle, position, or policy taught or advocated, as of a religion or government. For our purposes here, we will define it as a set of principles. The 8 principles that we will cover here comprise a solid foundation of Christian Doctrine for you as you grow in grace.

<u>Lesson One: The Bible</u>

The Holy Bible was written by men divinely inspired (theopneustos/God-breathed) and is God's revelation of Himself to man. It is a perfect treasure of divine instruction. That is, having God for its author, salvation for its end, and truth, without any mixture of error, for its content, all Scripture is totally true and trustworthy. The Bible reveals the principles by which God judges us, and therefore is, and will remain to the end of the world the true center of Christian union, and the supreme standard by which all human conduct, creeds, and religious opinions should be tried. All Scripture is a testimony to Christ, who is Himself the focus of divine revelation. **Special note: anything which purports itself to be Scripture or equal thereto but does not give Christ His proper glory is not Scripture but is actually not more than blasphemous trash.** The entirety of Scripture has one overarching goal, to glorify Christ by displaying Him, in His fullness.
In the original autographs (manuscripts) we say that the Bible is
1.   Inspired (God-breathed/authored)
1.   Inerrant (no errors, no contradictions)
1.   Infallible (cannot fail)
Special Note: The Bible stands alone as our authority. We submit to its authority because it is Divinely Inspired. There are no additional testaments etc. needed.

As part of the Doctrine of the Bible, we teach the verbal, plenary inspiration of Scripture. When we say that we mean that every word of the Scripture is inspired by the Holy Spirit. Every word that is found in the original autographs is there because God wills for it to be so. When we say plenary, we mean that each portion of the Bible is fully authoritative. Both the Old Testament and the New Testament are equally inspired and therefore of value to the Christian. If you remember the Emmaus Road Experience (Luke 24:13-35), you will remember that Jesus began with Moses and the Prophets and interpreted all things in the Scriptures concerning Himself. Moses and the Prophets is a euphemistic way of referring to the Old Testament.

What does the Bible say about the Bible?

2 Timothy 3:16-17 is where we get the idea that the Bible is God-breathed and profitable for

1. Doctrine
1. Reproof
1. Correction
1. Instruction in righteousness

Supporting Scriptures

2 Peter 1:19-21, 1 Peter 1:23-25, Psalm 19:7-12, Luke 21:33, Hebrews 4:12, Romans 1:16, John 1:1-4, 14, Hebrews 1:1-13, Titus 1:2

Overview of the books of the Bible

1. The Bible contains 66 books: 39 in the Old Testament and 27 in the New Testament written by over 40 "authors" over 1800 years
1. The books are divided into chapters and verses for reference and navigation.
1. The Old Testament was written in the Hebrew language.
1. The New Testament was written in the Greek language and our English Bible is a translation from these original languages.

Looking at the Bible from an academic perspective, we see that there are 2 Ways to order the canonical books: (Canonical = authorized)

"Normal" English Bible reflecting Greek/Western thought and style:

1. The Pentateuch/Law: Genesis through Deuteronomy
1. History: Joshua through Esther
1. Poetry and Wisdom: Job through The Song of Solomon
1. Prophets: Isaiah through Malachi
1. Gospels: Matthew through John
1. History: Acts of the Holy Spirit
1. Epistles/Letters: Romans through Philemon
1. The "Catholic/General" Epistles: Hebrews through Jude
1. The Apocalypse: Revelation

The 2nd way to order the canonical books are to follow the order of the Jewish Bible. The two sections of the Jewish Bible are TaNaKH and B'rit Hadashah TaNaKH is Torah (Teaching) Nevi'im (Prophets) and K'tuvim (Writings) This order is not considered to be essential to salvation but some may find it interesting as this is the Bible Jesus and the Apostles used
In TaNaKH order the Books are as follows:

Torah
B'resheet (Genesis), Sh'mot (Exodus), Vayikra (Leviticus), B'midbar (Numbers but literally, Wanderings), D'varim (Deuteronomy)

Nevi'im Rishonim (Early Prophets)
Y'hoshua (Joshua), Shof'tim (Judges), Sh'mu'el Alef (1 Samuel), Sh'mu'el Bet (2 Samuel), M'lakhim Alef (1 Kings), M'lakhim Bet (2 Kings)

Nevi'im Acharonim (Later Prophets)
Yesha'yahu (Isaiah), Yiremeyahu (Jeremiah), Yechezk'el, Shinem-'asar (the 12. In Hebrew Scripture these comprise a single book) Hoshea (Hosea), Yo'el (Joel), 'Amos (Amos), Ovadyah (Obadiah), Yonah (Jonah), Mikha (Micah), Nachum (Nahum), Havakuk (Habakkuk), Tz'fanyah (Zephaniah), Hagai (Haggai), Z'kharyah (Zechariah), Mal'akhi (Malachai)

K'tuvim (Writings)
Tehillim (Psalms), Mishlei (Proverbs), Iyov (Job)
The 5 Megillot (Scrolls)
Shir-Hashirim (Song of Songs), Rut (Ruth), Eikhah (Lamentations), Kohelet (Ecclesiastes), Ester (Esther), Dani'el (Daniel), Ezra-Nechemyah (Ezra-Nehemiah), Divrei-Ha Yamim Alef (1 Chronicles), Divrei-Ha Yahim Bet (2 Chronicles)

Like other forms of literature, there are types of Scripture
1. Historical Narrative: narrative that lays foundation for future things
1. Poetical: song-like, worshipful or proverbial
1. Prophetical: can be the Word describing future events but more importantly, authoritative communication on behalf of the Lord God. At times, the Prophetic can be polemical in nature, such as when denouncing false prophets.
1. Instructional: practical application of Scripture

Interpreting the Bible
Each passage of Scripture only has 1 correct interpretation, but how do we arrive at that? Start by reading like any other book. No that wasn't a disrespectful statement…
5 Principles for Interpretation
1. **Literal Principle**: We interpret the Bible according to the normal rules of language. We are not looking for some secret "super spiritual" meaning. Normal people wrote using normal language. Metaphors, similes, analogies, etc. These all follow the normal rules just as they would anywhere else. Figures of speech are normal language. Symbolism is normal language.

But allegory is secret, hidden meaning that is not contained in the normal language. **There are no allegories in the Bible. There are no allegories, whatsoever, in the Bible; it is normal language, it means exactly what it appears to mean.** There is no deeper meaning, there's no hidden meaning, there's no secret meaning, there's no spiritualized meaning. Yes, there are prophetic passages where there are analogies; these are illustrations. You read Zechariah, Daniel, Ezekiel, Isaiah, and in the book of Revelation you see images…those images are conveying a reality. They are conveying a reality in a symbolic way. Even Jesus used differing types of language. Case in point: parables. Parables were fictional stories conveying actual truth.

1.   **Historical Principle**: culture, geography, politics, religion, the thinking of the people, the perspectives, the world view, what's going on at the time, how the people think…all of that is informing you on the historical context. (I won't make many product endorsements but the Bible Background Commentary from InterVarsity Press is an outstanding resource for this.)

1.   **Grammatical Principle** (Quoting John MacArthur)"This is to take a look at the language and the syntax and lexicography of a passage…the words, the way they're arranged, the prepositions, the pronouns, the antecedents. And you can do that in your English Bible. What do the words mean? What does the antecedent of this? What is the preposition telling me? To what does this pronoun refer? To whom does it refer? So it's a grammatical thing. We break that into word studies, studies of actual words, syntax which is how the words are connected with each other."

1.   **Synthesis Principle:** The Reformers used the expression Scriptrua Scripturum Intepretatur or in English, the Scripture interprets the Scripture. Two of my dear friends like to refer to the New Testament as a commentary on the Old Testament and it certainly is. Example: Sermon on the Mount is expository treatment of many OT Laws

1.   **Practical Principle** What are the implications of the text? What is the truth that was delivered and what do I do with it?

There are so many English Bibles, which one should I choose?
This is one of the most important decisions you will ever make, Beloved. The advice below should prove helpful to selecting which Bible will be your primary.
Choose a Bible that is as literal as possible but still easy to understand. Ideally, you want to use an essentially literal (form-based/word for word) translation. I use three, primarily: The New American Standard Bible (of which the 1977 edition is the most literal English edition made), The English Standard Version (primarily for teaching because of its global availability) and the Holman Christian Standard Bible. Other English versions that would be very literal are the King James Version, New King James Version. Many people regularly me ask if a thought for thought/dynamic equivalence translation is ok and what they mean is, "is it acceptable to use the NIV or NLT Versions, or perhaps

something similar?" Yes. It may have some deficiencies, such as not translating the words exactly, but you will still be able to have successful study. English versions in this category are the New Living Translation, New International Version, New English Translation, Revised English Bible. Paraphrases like the Message and the Voice should be avoided at all cost since we are not looking for opinion on what the text says.

Choose a Bible that is designed for study. If you are able, you should get a wide margin Bible. As you study the Holy Spirit will bring things to mind that you will want to remember for a long time and a wide margin is an excellent choice here. A Bible with cross references is also an excellent choice, especially where the synthesis principle comes in. The references will be a guide to using the Bible to interpret itself. Some will come with commentary pre-included. This is ok but you really ought to put in the labor for your own study.

Most importantly, get the same translation that your primary pastor uses. (You may listen to many teachers but you need to use the version that is read in the pulpit where you attend church. You will find that it helps you understand better because you will have cohesion with the members of your church and will be able to discuss the text.

I have chosen my Bible and I learned how to interpret it. Now what?

The best way to study your Bible is to use the method known as Inductive Study

Our colleagues at Precept Ministries (http://precept.org) have some excellent wisdom on the Inductive Study Method

"Begin with Prayer

Prayer is often the missing element in Bible study. You are about to learn the most effective method of Bible study there is. Yet apart from the work of the Holy Spirit, that's all it will be—a method.

Ask the "5 W's and an H"

As you study any passage of Scripture, train yourself to constantly ask: **Who?**

What? When? Where? Why? How? These questions are the building blocks of precise **observation,** which is essential for accurate **interpretation.**

Mark key words and phrases

A key word is one that is essential to the text. Key words and phrases are repeated in order to convey the author's point or purpose for writing. For example, notice that some form of the word *suffering* is used three times in 1 Peter 5. Key words can be marked using symbols, colors, or a combination of the two.

Make lists

Making lists can be one of the most enlightening things you do as you study. Lists reveal truths and highlight important concepts. 1 Peter 5:2,3, for example, contains a simple list regarding the role of the elder, shown by numbering the items in the text. It is also helpful to make a list of what you learn about each key word or person you mark.

Watch for contrasts and comparisons
Contrasts and comparisons use highly descriptive language to make it easier to remember what you've learned. For example, Peter compares the devil to a roaring lion in verse 8. Peter also contrasts God's attitude toward the proud and the humble.

Note expressions of time
The relationship of events in time often sheds light on the true meaning of the text. Marking them will help you see the sequence or timing of events and lead to accurate interpretation of Scripture.

Geographic Locations
Often it's helpful to mark geographical locations, which tell you where an event takes place.

Mark terms of conclusion
Words such as "therefore," "thus," and "for this reason" indicate that a conclusion or summary is being made. You may want to underline them in the text.

Identify chapter themes
The theme of a chapter will center on the main person, event, teaching, or subject of that section of Scripture. Themes are often revealed by reviewing the key words and lists you developed. Try to express the theme as briefly as possible, using words found in the text.

Remember that context rules.
If you lay the solid foundation of observation, you will be prepared to consider each verse in the light of the surrounding verses, the book in which it is found, and the entire Word of God. As you study, ask yourself: Is my interpretation of this passage of Scripture consistent with the theme, purpose, and structure of the book in which it is found? Is it consistent with other Scripture about the same subject? Am I considering the historic and cultural context? Never take a Scripture out of its context to make it say what you want it to say. Discover what the author is saying; don't add to his meaning.

Always seek the full counsel of the Word of God.
When you know God's Word thoroughly, you will not accept a teaching

simply because someone has used one or two isolated verses to support it. You will be able to discern whether a teaching is biblical or not. Saturate yourself in the Word of God; it is your safeguard against wrong doctrine.

Remember that Scripture will never contradict Scripture.
Remember, all Scripture is inspired by God. Therefore, Scripture will never contradict itself. Sometimes, however, you may find it difficult to reconcile two seemingly contradictory truths taught in Scripture, such as the sovereignty of God and the responsibility of man. Don't take a teaching to an extreme that God doesn't. Simply humble your heart in faith and believe what God says, even if you can't fully understand or reconcile it at the moment.

Don't base your convictions on an obscure passage of Scripture.
An obscure passage is one in which the meaning is unclear or not easily understood. Because these passages are difficult to understand even when proper principles of interpretation are used, they should not be used as a basis for establishing doctrine.

Interpret Scripture literally.
God spoke to us that we might know truth. Therefore, take the Word of God at face value—in its natural, normal sense. Look first for the clear teaching of Scripture, not a hidden meaning. Understand and recognize figures of speech and interpret them accordingly.

Consider what is being said in the light of its literary style. For example, you will find more similes and metaphors in poetical and prophetic literature than in historical or biographical books. Interpret portions of Scripture according to their literary style.
Some literary styles in the Bible are: Historical—Acts, Exodus; Prophetic—Revelation, Isaiah; Biographical—Luke; Didactic (teaching)—Romans; Poetic—Psalms; Epistle (letter)—2 Timothy; Proverbial—Proverbs

Look for the single meaning of the passage.
Always try to understand what the author had in mind when you interpret a portion of the Bible. Don't twist verses to support a meaning that is not clearly taught. Unless the author of a particular book indicates that there is another meaning to what he says, let the passage speak for itself."

It has been mentioned that the Bible is inerrant. To explore that a little further, we are providing the Chicago Statement on Biblical Inerrancy
The Chicago Statement on Biblical Inerrancy

Preface

The authority of Scripture is a key issue for the Christian church in this and every age. Those who profess faith in Jesus Christ as Lord and Savior are called to show the reality of their discipleship by humbly and faithfully obeying God's written Word. To stray from Scripture in faith or conduct is disloyalty to our Master. Recognition of the total truth and trustworthiness of Holy Scripture is essential to a full grasp and adequate confession of its authority.

The following Statement affirms this inerrancy of Scripture afresh, making clear our understanding of it and warning against its denial. We are persuaded that to deny it is to set aside the witness of Jesus Christ and of the Holy Spirit and to refuse that submission to the claims of God's own Word which marks true Christian faith. We see it as our timely duty to make this affirmation in the face of current lapses from the truth of inerrancy among our fellow Christians and misunderstandings of this doctrine in the world at large.

This Statement consists of three parts: a Summary Statement, Articles of Affirmation and Denial, and an accompanying Exposition. It has been prepared in the course of a three-day consultation in Chicago. Those who have signed the Summary Statement and the Articles wish to affirm their own conviction as to the inerrancy of Scripture and to encourage and challenge one another and all Christians to growing appreciation and understanding of this doctrine. We acknowledge the limitations of a document prepared in a brief, intensive conference and do not propose that this Statement be given creedal weight. Yet we rejoice in the deepening of our own convictions through our discussions together, and we pray that the Statement we have signed may be used to the glory of our God toward a new reformation of the Church in its faith, life, and mission.

We offer this Statement in a spirit, not of contention, but of humility and love, which we purpose by God's grace to maintain in any future dialogue arising out of what we have said. We gladly acknowledge that many who deny the inerrancy of Scripture do not display the consequences of this denial in the rest of their belief and behavior, and we are conscious that we who confess this doctrine often deny it in life by failing to bring our thoughts and deeds, our traditions and habits, into true subjection to the divine Word.

We invite response to this statement from any who see reason to amend its affirmations about Scripture by the light of Scripture itself, under whose infallible authority we stand as we speak. We claim no personal infallibility for the witness we bear, and for any help which enables us to strengthen this testimony to God's Word we shall be grateful.
— The Draft Committee

A Short Statement

1. God, who is Himself Truth and speaks truth only, has inspired Holy Scripture in order thereby to reveal Himself to lost mankind through Jesus Christ as Creator and Lord, Redeemer and Judge. Holy Scripture is God's witness to Himself.

2. Holy Scripture, being God's own Word, written by men prepared and superintended by His Spirit, is of infallible divine authority in all matters upon which it touches: it is to be believed, as God's instruction, in all that it affirms: obeyed, as God's command, in all that it requires; embraced, as God's pledge, in all that it promises.

3. The Holy Spirit, Scripture's divine Author, both authenticates it to us by His inward witness and opens our minds to understand its meaning.

4. Being wholly and verbally God-given, Scripture is without error or fault in all its teaching, no less in what it states about God's acts in creation, about the events of world history, and about its own literary origins under God, than in its witness to God's saving grace in individual lives.

5. The authority of Scripture is inescapably impaired if this total divine inerrancy is in any way limited or disregarded, or made relative to a view of truth contrary to the Bible's own; and such lapses bring serious loss to both the individual and the Church.

Articles of Affirmation and Denial

Article I.
WE AFFIRM that the Holy Scriptures are to be received as the authoritative Word of God.
WE DENY that the Scriptures receive their authority from the Church, tradition, or any other human source.

Article II.
WE AFFIRM that the Scriptures are the supreme written norm by which God binds the conscience, and that the authority of the Church is subordinate to that of Scripture.
WE DENY that Church creeds, councils, or declarations have authority greater than or equal to the authority of the Bible.

Article III.
WE AFFIRM that the written Word in its entirety is revelation given by God.

WE DENY that the Bible is merely a witness to revelation, or only becomes revelation in encounter, or depends on the responses of men for its validity.

Article IV.
WE AFFIRM that God who made mankind in His image has used language as a means of revelation.
WE DENY that human language is so limited by our creatureliness that it is rendered inadequate as a vehicle for divine revelation. We further deny that the corruption of human culture and language through sin has thwarted God's work of inspiration.

Article V.
WE AFFIRM that God's revelation within the Holy Scriptures was progressive.
WE DENY that later revelation, which may fulfill earlier revelation, ever corrects or contradicts it. We further deny that any normative revelation has been given since the completion of the New Testament writings.

Article VI.
WE AFFIRM that the whole of Scripture and all its parts, down to the very words of the original, were given by divine inspiration.
WE DENY that the inspiration of Scripture can rightly be affirmed of the whole without the parts, or of some parts but not the whole.

Article VII.
WE AFFIRM that inspiration was the work in which God by His Spirit, through human writers, gave us His Word. The origin of Scripture is divine. The mode of divine inspiration remains largely a mystery to us.
WE DENY that inspiration can be reduced to human insight, or to heightened states of consciousness of any kind.

Article VIII.
WE AFFIRM that God in His work of inspiration utilized the distinctive personalities and literary styles of the writers whom He had chosen and prepared.
WE DENY that God, in causing these writers to use the very words that He chose, overrode their personalities.

Article IX.
WE AFFIRM that inspiration, though not conferring omniscience, guaranteed true and trustworthy utterance on all matters of which the Biblical authors were moved to speak and write.
WE DENY that the finitude or fallenness of these writers, by necessity or otherwise, introduced distortion or falsehood into God's Word.

Article X.

WE AFFIRM that inspiration, strictly speaking, applies only to the autographic text of Scripture, which in the providence of God can be ascertained from available manuscripts with great accuracy. We further affirm that copies and translations of Scripture are the Word of God to the extent that they faithfully represent the original.

WE DENY that any essential element of the Christian faith is affected by the absence of the autographs. We further deny that this absence renders the assertion of Biblical inerrancy invalid or irrelevant.

Article XI.

WE AFFIRM that Scripture, having been given by divine inspiration, is infallible, so that, far from misleading us, it is true and reliable in all the matters it addresses.

WE DENY that it is possible for the Bible to be at the same time infallible and errant in its assertions. Infallibility and inerrancy may be distinguished, but not separated.

Article XII.

WE AFFIRM that Scripture in its entirety is inerrant, being free from all falsehood, fraud, or deceit.

WE DENY that Biblical infallibility and inerrancy are limited to spiritual, religious, or redemptive themes, exclusive of assertions in the fields of history and science. We further deny that scientific hypotheses about earth history may properly be used to overturn the teaching of Scripture on creation and the flood.

Article XIII.

WE AFFIRM the propriety of using inerrancy as a theological term with reference to the complete truthfulness of Scripture.

WE DENY that it is proper to evaluate Scripture according to standards of truth and error that are alien to its usage or purpose. We further deny that inerrancy is negated by Biblical phenomena such as a lack of modern technical precision, irregularities of grammar or spelling, observational descriptions of nature, the reporting of falsehoods, the use of hyperbole and round numbers, the topical arrangement of material, variant selections of material in parallel accounts, or the use of free citations.

Article XIV.

WE AFFIRM the unity and internal consistency of Scripture.

WE DENY that alleged errors and discrepancies that have not yet been resolved vitiate the truth claims of the Bible.

Article XV.
WE AFFIRM that the doctrine of inerrancy is grounded in the teaching of the Bible about inspiration.

WE DENY that Jesus' teaching about Scripture may be dismissed by appeals to accommodation or to any natural limitation of His humanity.

Article XVI.
WE AFFIRM that the doctrine of inerrancy has been integral to the Church's faith throughout its history.

WE DENY that inerrancy is a doctrine invented by scholastic Protestantism, or is a reactionary position postulated in response to negative higher criticism.

Article XVII.
WE AFFIRM that the Holy Spirit bears witness to the Scriptures, assuring believers of the truthfulness of God's written Word.

WE DENY that this witness of the Holy Spirit operates in isolation from or against Scripture.

Article XVIII.
WE AFFIRM that the text of Scripture is to be interpreted by grammatico-historical exegesis, taking account of its literary forms and devices, and that Scripture is to interpret Scripture.

WE DENY the legitimacy of any treatment of the text or quest for sources lying behind it that leads to relativizing, dehistoricizing, or discounting its teaching, or rejecting its claims to authorship.

Article XIX.
WE AFFIRM that a confession of the full authority, infallibility, and inerrancy of Scripture is vital to a sound understanding of the whole of the Christian faith. We further affirm that such confession should lead to increasing conformity to the image of Christ.

WE DENY that such confession is necessary for salvation. However, we further deny that inerrancy can be rejected without grave consequences, both to the individual and to the Church.

Exposition

Our understanding of the doctrine of inerrancy must be set in the context of the broader teachings of the Scripture concerning itself. This exposition gives an account of the outline of doctrine from which our summary statement and articles are drawn.

Creation, Revelation and Inspiration
The Triune God, who formed all things by his creative utterances and governs all things by His Word of decree, made mankind in His own image for a life of

communion with Himself, on the model of the eternal fellowship of loving communication within the Godhead. As God's image-bearer, man was to hear God's Word addressed to him and to respond in the joy of adoring obedience. Over and above God's self-disclosure in the created order and the sequence of events within it, human beings from Adam on have received verbal messages from Him, either directly, as stated in Scripture, or indirectly in the form of part or all of Scripture itself.

When Adam fell, the Creator did not abandon mankind to final judgment but promised salvation and began to reveal Himself as Redeemer in a sequence of historical events centering on Abraham's family and culminating in the life, death, resurrection, present heavenly ministry, and promised return of Jesus Christ. Within this frame God has from time to time spoken specific words of judgment and mercy, promise and command, to sinful human beings so drawing them into a covenant relation of mutual commitment between Him and them in which He blesses them with gifts of grace and they bless Him in responsive adoration. Moses, whom God used as mediator to carry His words to His people at the time of the Exodus, stands at the head of a long line of prophets in whose mouths and writings God put His words for delivery to Israel. God's purpose in this succession of messages was to maintain His covenant by causing His people to know His Name—that is, His nature—and His will both of precept and purpose in the present and for the future. This line of prophetic spokesmen from God came to completion in Jesus Christ, God's incarnate Word, who was Himself a prophet—more than a prophet, but not less—and in the apostles and prophets of the first Christian generation. When God's final and climactic message, His word to the world concerning Jesus Christ, had been spoken and elucidated by those in the apostolic circle, the sequence of revealed messages ceased. Henceforth the Church was to live and know God by what He had already said, and said for all time.

At Sinai God wrote the terms of His covenant on tables of stone, as His enduring witness and for lasting accessibility, and throughout the period of prophetic and apostolic revelation He prompted men to write the messages given to and through them, along with celebratory records of His dealings with His people, plus moral reflections on covenant life and forms of praise and prayer for covenant mercy. The theological reality of inspiration in the producing of Biblical documents corresponds to that of spoken prophecies: although the human writers' personalities were expressed in what they wrote, the words were divinely constituted. Thus, what Scripture says, God says; its authority is His authority, for He is its ultimate Author, having given it through the minds and words of chosen and prepared men who in freedom and faithfulness "spoke from God as they were carried along by the Holy Spirit" (2 Pet. 1:21). Holy Scripture must be acknowledged as the Word of God by virtue of its divine origin.

Authority: Christ and the Bible

Jesus Christ, the Son of God who is the Word made flesh, our Prophet, Priest, and King, is the ultimate Mediator of God's communication to man, as He is of all God's gifts of grace. The revelation He gave was more than verbal; He revealed the Father by His presence and His deeds as well. Yet His words were crucially important; for He was God, He spoke from the Father, and His words will judge all men at the last day.

As the prophesied Messiah, Jesus Christ is the central theme of Scripture. The Old Testament looked ahead to Him; the New Testament looks back to His first coming and on to His second. Canonical Scripture is the divinely inspired and therefore normative witness to Christ. No hermeneutic, therefore, of which the historical Christ is not the focal point is acceptable. Holy Scripture must be treated as what it essentially is—the witness of the Father to the Incarnate Son.

It appears that the Old Testament canon had been fixed by the time of Jesus. The New Testament canon is likewise now closed inasmuch as no new apostolic witness to the historical Christ can now be borne. No new revelation (as distinct from Spirit-given understanding of existing revelation) will be given until Christ comes again. The canon was created in principle by divine inspiration. The Church's part was to discern the canon which God had created, not to devise one of its own.

The word *canon,* signifying a rule or standard, is a pointer to authority, which means the right to rule and control. Authority in Christianity belongs to God in His revelation, which means, on the one hand, Jesus Christ, the living Word, and, on the other hand, Holy Scripture, the written Word. But the authority of Christ and that of Scripture are one. As our Prophet, Christ testified that Scripture cannot be broken. As our Priest and King, He devoted His earthly life to fulfilling the law and the prophets, even dying in obedience to the words of Messianic prophecy. Thus, as He saw Scripture attesting Him and His authority, so by His own submission to Scripture He attested its authority. As He bowed to His Father's instruction given in His Bible (our Old Testament), so He requires His disciples to do—not, however, in isolation but in conjunction with the apostolic witness to Himself which He undertook to inspire by His gift of the Holy Spirit. So Christians show themselves faithful servants of their Lord by bowing to the divine instruction given in the prophetic and apostolic writings which together make up our Bible.

By authenticating each other's authority, Christ and Scripture coalesce into a single fount of authority. The Biblically-interpreted Christ and the Christ-centered, Christ-proclaiming Bible are from this standpoint one. As from the fact of inspiration we infer that what Scripture says, God says, so from the

revealed relation between Jesus Christ and Scripture we may equally declare
that what Scripture says, Christ says.

Infallibility, Inerrancy, Interpretation

Holy Scripture, as the inspired Word of God witnessing authoritatively to
Jesus Christ, may properly be called *infallible* and *inerrant*. These negative
terms have a special value, for they explicitly safeguard crucial positive truths.
Infallible signifies the quality of neither misleading nor being misled and so
safeguards in categorical terms the truth that Holy Scripture is a sure, safe, and
reliable rule and guide in all matters.

Similarly, *inerrant* signifies the quality of being free from all falsehood or
mistake and so safeguards the truth that Holy Scripture is entirely true and
trustworthy in all its assertions.

We affirm that canonical Scripture should always be interpreted on the basis
that it is infallible and inerrant. However, in determining what the God-taught
writer is asserting in each passage, we must pay the most careful attention to
its claims and character as a human production. In inspiration, God utilized the
culture and conventions of His penman's milieu, a milieu that God controls in
His sovereign providence; it is misinterpretation to imagine otherwise.

So history must be treated as history, poetry as poetry, hyperbole and
metaphor as hyperbole and metaphor, generalization and approximation as
what they are, and so forth. Differences between literary conventions in Bible
times and in ours must also be observed: since, for instance, non-chronological
narration and imprecise citation were conventional and acceptable and violated
no expectations in those days, we must not regard these things as faults when
we find them in Bible writers. When total precision of a particular kind was
not expected nor aimed at, it is no error not to have achieved it. Scripture is
inerrant, not in the sense of being absolutely precise by modern standards, but
in the sense of making good its claims and achieving that measure of focused
truth at which its authors aimed.

**The truthfulness of Scripture is not negated by the appearance in it of
irregularities of grammar or spelling, phenomenal descriptions of nature,
reports of false statements (*e.g.*, the lies of Satan), or seeming
discrepancies between one passage and another. It is not right to set the
so-called "phenomena" of Scripture against the teaching of Scripture
about itself. Apparent inconsistencies should not be ignored. Solution of
them, where this can be convincingly achieved, will encourage our faith,
and where for the present no convincing solution is at hand we shall
significantly honor God by trusting His assurance that His Word is true,
despite these appearances, and by maintaining our confidence that one
day they will be seen to have been illusions. (Emphasis Added)**

Inasmuch as all Scripture is the product of a single divine mind, interpretation
must stay within the bounds of the analogy of Scripture and eschew
hypotheses that would correct one Biblical passage by another, whether in the

name of progressive revelation or of the imperfect enlightenment of the inspired writer's mind.

Although Holy Scripture is nowhere culture-bound in the sense that its teaching lacks universal validity, it is sometimes culturally conditioned by the customs and conventional views of a particular period, so that the application of its principles today calls for a different sort of action.

Skepticism and Criticism

Since the Renaissance, and more particularly since the Enlightenment, world-views have been developed which involve skepticism about basic Christian tenets. Such are the agnosticism which denies that God is knowable, the rationalism which denies that He is incomprehensible, the idealism which denies that He is transcendent, and the existentialism which denies rationality in His relationships with us. When these un- and anti-biblical principles seep into men's theologies at presuppositional level, as today they frequently do, faithful interpretation of Holy Scripture becomes impossible.

Transmission and Translation

Since God has nowhere promised an inerrant transmission of Scripture, it is necessary to affirm that only the autographic text of the original documents was inspired and to maintain the need of textual criticism as a means of detecting any slips that may have crept into the text in the course of its transmission. The verdict of this science, however, is that the Hebrew and Greek text appear to be amazingly well preserved, so that we are amply justified in affirming, with the Westminster Confession, a singular providence of God in this matter and in declaring that the authority of Scripture is in no way jeopardized by the fact that the copies we possess are not entirely error-free.

Similarly, no translation is or can be perfect, and all translations are an additional step away from the *autographa*. Yet the verdict of linguistic science is that English-speaking Christians, at least, are exceedingly well served in these days with a host of excellent translations and have no cause for hesitating to conclude that the true Word of God is within their reach. Indeed, in view of the frequent repetition in Scripture of the main matters with which it deals and also of the Holy Spirit's constant witness to and through the Word, no serious translation of Holy Scripture will so destroy its meaning as to render it unable to make its reader "wise for salvation through faith in Christ Jesus" (2 Tim. 3:15).

Inerrancy and Authority

In our affirmation of the authority of Scripture as involving its total truth, we are consciously standing with Christ and His apostles, indeed with the whole Bible and with the main stream of Church history from the first days until very recently. We are concerned at the casual, inadvertent, and seemingly thoughtless way in which a belief of such far-reaching importance has been given up by so many in our day.

We are conscious too that great and grave confusion results from ceasing to maintain the total truth of the Bible whose authority one professes to acknowledge. The result of taking this step is that the Bible which God gave loses its authority, and what has authority instead is a Bible reduced in content according to the demands of one's critical reasonings and in principle reducible still further once one has started. This means that at bottom independent reason now has authority, as opposed to Scriptural teaching. If this is not seen and if for the time being basic evangelical doctrines are still held, persons denying the full truth of Scripture may claim an evangelical identity while methodologically they have moved away from the evangelical principle of knowledge to an unstable subjectivism, and will find it hard not to move further.

We affirm that what Scripture says, God says. May He be glorified. Amen and Amen."

Lesson 2: The One True God

The Bible Assumes the Existence of God. Throughout the Scripture we see the assumption of the existence of God and the fact that He predates all things and is without cause. The Bible never attempts to prove the existence of God; it simply assumes He is.

For Reference:

Genesis 1:1, John 1:1, Psalm 19:1, Psalm 90:2

In the Bible, we see that God reveals His Name as I AM (Exodus 3:14). In Hebrew it is Ehyeh Aser Ehyeh. This can be translated as I am who I am, I will be what I will be, or even I am because I am. Though Biblical Hebrew does not have verb tenses, the English translation of the Name is in the Present Continuous Tense. This is an allusion to the fact that God is unbound by time. We can also say this is an allusion to God as the "uncaused cause of all things."

In the the Bible God is, frequently, explained through His Names which define or explain God by what He is and what He does. Here are some examples:

1. El, Elim, Elohim, Eloah: deity (Genesis 1:1)
1. Adonai: my Lord (as of a servant to a master)
1. El-Elyon: the most high (Psalm 78:35)
1. El-Shaddai: Almighty God (Genesis 17:1)
1. YHWH (believed to be pronounced yah way): the personal name of God. This is the 2nd Person Derivative of the I AM WHO I AM name "to be, the one who causes to be, self-existent one" (Exodus 3:14)
1. YHWH-Jireh: the Lord will provide (Genesis 22:14)
1. YHWH-Rophe: the Lord that heals (Exodus 15:26)

1.	YHWH-Nissi: the Lord our banner/protection (Exodus 17:15)
1.	YHWH-Shalom: the Lord our peace (Judges 6:24)
1.	YHWH-Raah: the Lord my Shepherd (Psalm 23:1)
1.	YHWH-Tsidkenu: the Lord our righteousness (Jeremiah 23:6)
1.	YHWH-Shammah: the Lord is present (Ezekiel 48:35)
1.	YHWH Sabaoth-The Lord of hosts (Psalm 89:6-8, James 5:4)
1.	YHWH Mekkodishkim- The Lord who makes us holy/sanctifies (Exodus 31:130
1.	El HaNe'eman- The Faithful God: (Deuteronomy 7:9).
1.	El HaGadol- The Great God: (Deuteronomy 10:17).
1.	El HaKadosh- The Holy God: (Isaiah 5:16).
1.	El Yisrael- The God Of Israel: (Psalm 68:35).
1.	El HaShamayim- The God Of The Heavens: (Psalm 136:26).
1.	El De'ot- The God Of Knowledge: (1 Samuel 2:3).
1.	El Emet- The God Of Truth: (Psalm 31:6).
1.	El Yeshuati- The God Of My Salvation: (Isaiah 12:2).
1.	El Elyon- The Most High God: (Genesis 14:18).
1.	Immanu El- God Is With Us: (Isaiah 7:14).
1.	El Olam- The God Of Eternity (Genesis 21:33).
1.	El Echad- The One God: (Malachi 2:10). "
1.	Elah Yerush'lem- God of Jerusalem: (Ezra 7:19).
1.	Elah Yisrael- God of Israel: (Ezra 5:1).
1.	Elah Sh'maya- God of Heaven: (Ezra 7:23).
1.	Elah Sh'maya V'Arah- God of Heaven and Earth: (Ezra 5:11).

We now come to a fairly obvious question: Is there evidence for the existence of God outside of the Bible? Romans 1 points out that creation declares the glory of God. We also have the conscience, a moral compass so to speak that is built into every person. Additionally, there are the arguments from, Teleology, Cosmology, and Logic, all of which we will cover in our next chapter, the Lesson on God the Father.

As we are discussing the Godhead, there is an essential doctrine, meaning that the Church Fathers considered this a salvation issue, that must be treated, the Trinity.

The Lord God has revealed Himself as embodying relationship and association in that He exists as Father, Son, and Holy Ghost.

Scriptures which infer the Trinity:

Deuteronomy 6:4, Isaiah 43:10,11, Matthew 28:19, Luke 3:22

It is true that the terms "Trinity" and "persons" as related to God are not found in the Scriptures, but they are words in harmony with Scripture. Since this doctrine is a logical consequence of a study of the Bible, we say they are harmonious with the Scripture. He is, therefore, distinguished from "gods many and lords many." We therefore may speak of Lord our God who is One

Lord, as a trinity or as one Being of three persons, and still be absolutely scriptural.
Matthew 28:19, 2 Corinthians 13:14, John 14:16-17

Distinction of Persons and Relationship in the Trinity
Jesus taught a distinction of Persons in the Godhead, which He expressed in specific terms of relationship, as Father, Son, and Holy Spirit. We need to point out that this distinction and relationship, as to its mode, is inscrutable and incomprehensible, because it is never fully explained. This is, indeed, one of the great mysteries of the Christian Faith.
Luke 1:35, 1 Corinthians 1:24, Matthew 11:25-27, Matthew 28:19, 2 Corinthians 13:14, 1 John 1:3-4

Unity of the One Being of Father, Son and Holy Spirit
In the Shema, Deuteronomy 6:4, we see that God is referred to with the word echad, a word which designates a compound unity as opposed to yachid, which would designate a singular unity. *I do need to point out that while we believe that there are 3 distinct Persons in the Godhead, we do not believe or teach that there are 3 different Gods. The Trinity remains a mystery that we will not fully understand until we are in Heaven...*There is that in the Father which constitutes Him as the Father and not the Son; there is that in the Son which constitutes Him the Son and not the Father; and there is that in the Holy Spirit which constitutes Him the Holy Spirit and not either the Father or the Son.
John 1:18, John 15:26, John 17:11, John 17:21, Zechariah 14:9

Identity and Cooperation in the Godhead
The Father, the Son and the Holy Spirit are never identical as to Person; nor are they confused as to relation; nor divided in respect to being God; nor opposed as to cooperation. The Son is in the Father and the Father is in the Son as to relationship. The Son is with the Father and the Father is with the Son, as to fellowship. The Father is not from the Son, but the Son is from the Father, as to authority. The Holy Spirit is from the Father and the Son proceeding, as to nature, relationship, cooperation and authority. Therefore, no Person in the Godhead either exists or works separately or independently of the others.
John 5:17-30, John 5:32, John 5:37, John 8:17,18

Is this really a historically orthodox doctrine? Did the Church Fathers really believe in the Trinity? Yes. The Trinity is an historically catholic teaching of the Church and is, several times, seen the Epistolary Greetings of the Apostle Paul(as a reminder, when we refer to the "Catholic" Faith we do not mean the Roman Catholic Church; we mean the church universal). It was not without issue though. Two teachings arose quickly that were determined to be heretical by the Council of Nicaea, Arianism and Sabellianism. Interestingly enough to major groups exist today that continue to teach these heresies.

What is Arianism?

The modern version of Arianism is also known as Jehovah's Witnesses though Mormonism is also very Arian in its Christology.

Arianism developed around 320 in Alexandria, Egypt, and concerning the person of Christ and is named after Arius of Alexandria. This teaching was condemned by the First Council of Nicaea.

Arianism misunderstands references to Jesus' being tired (John 4:6) and not knowing the date of His return (Matthew 24:36). Yes, it is difficult to understand how God could be tired and/or not know something, but relegating Jesus to a created being is not the answer. Jesus was fully God, but He was also fully human; we refer to this as the hypostatic union. Since Jesus did not become a human being until the incarnation, His limitations as a human being have no impact on His divine nature or eternality.

A second major misinterpretation in Arianism is the meaning of "firstborn" (Romans 8:29; Colossians 1:15-20). Arians understand "firstborn" in these verses to mean that Jesus was "born" or "created" as the first act of creation. This is not the case. Jesus Himself proclaimed His self-existence and eternality (John 8:58; 10:30). John 1:1-2 tells us that Jesus was "in the beginning with God." In Bible times, the firstborn son of a family was held in great honor (Genesis 49:3; Exodus 11:5; 34:19; Numbers 3:40; Psalm 89:27; Jeremiah 31:9). It is in this sense that Jesus is God's firstborn. Jesus is the preeminent member of God's family. Jesus is the anointed one, the "Wonderful Counselor, Mighty God, Everlasting Father, Prince of Peace" (Isaiah 9:6).

After nearly a century of debate, at various early church councils, the Christian church officially denounced Arianism as a false doctrine. Since that time, Arianism has never been accepted as a viable doctrine of the Christian faith. As we said, earlier, Arianism has not died, however. It is alive and well in the forms of the Jehovah's Witnesses and the Mormons.

What is Sabellianism (gotquestions.org)?

"One of the most hotly debated theological issues in the early Christian church was the doctrine of the Trinity. How do God the Father, God the Son, and God the Holy Spirit relate to one another? How can there only be one God, but three Persons? (All of the various early heresies resulted from individuals overemphasizing or underemphasizing various aspects of the Godhead. Ultimately, all of these false views result from attempts by finite human beings to fully understand an infinite God (Romans 11:33-36)). This will be a fairly long answer treating Sabellianism, Modalism, and Monarchianism, which are just three of the numerous false views and are very similar in nature. Monarchianism had two primary forms, Dynamic Monarchianism and Modalistic Monarchianism. Dynamic Monarchianism is the view that Jesus was not, in His nature, God. It is the view that God existed in Jesus, just as

God exists in all of us, but that God existed in Jesus in a particularly powerful way. Jesus was God because God inhabited Him. Modalistic Monarchianism, also known as Modalism, is the view that God variously manifested Himself as the Father (primarily in the Old Testament), other times as the Son (primarily from Jesus' conception to His ascension), and other times as the Holy Spirit (primarily after Jesus' ascension into heaven). Modalistic Monarchianism / Modalism teaches that God has simply revealed Himself in three different modes, and that He is not three Persons, as the Bible asserts. Modalistic Monarchianism / Modalism is also known as Sabellianism, named after Sabellius, an influential early proponent of the view. Yet another aspect of Modalistic Monarchianism / Modalism / Sabellianism is Patripassianism, which is the view that it was God the Father who became incarnate, suffered, died, and was resurrected. Patripassianism essentially teaches that God the Father became His own Son. ***Note: Patripassinianism is frequently mocked by athiests who have a fundamental misunderstanding of the nature of God.*** Sabellianism, Modalism, Monarchianism (dynamic and modalistic), and Patripassianism are all unbiblical understandings of the relationship between the Persons of the Trinity. It is impossible for us as finite human beings to fully understand an infinite God. The Bible presents God as one God, but then speaks of three Persons—the Father, the Son, and the Holy Spirit. How these two truths harmonize is inconceivable to the human mind. When we attempt to define the indefinable (God), we will always fail to varying degrees. Dynamic Monarchianism fails in that it does not recognize the true deity of Jesus Christ. Modalistic Monarchianism / Modalism / Sabellianism / Patripassianism fails because it does not recognize God as three distinct Persons."

The Ecumenical Creeds, issued by the Church Councils answered the heretics:

The Apostles Creed

I believe in God, the Father Almighty, the Maker of heaven and earth, and in Jesus Christ, His only Son, our Lord: Who was conceived by the Holy Ghost, born of the virgin Mary, suffered under Pontius Pilate, was crucified, dead, and buried; He descended into hell. The third day He arose again from the dead; He ascended into heaven, and sitteth on the right hand of God the Father Almighty; from thence he shall come to judge the quick and the dead. I believe in the Holy Ghost; the holy catholic church; the communion of saints; the forgiveness of sins; the resurrection of the body; and the life everlasting. Amen.

Nicene Creed

I believe in one God, the Father Almighty, Maker of heaven and earth, and of all things visible and invisible. And in one Lord Jesus Christ, the only-begotten Son of God, begotten of the Father before all worlds; God of God, Light of Light, very God of very God; begotten, not made, being of one substance with the Father, by whom all things were made. Who, for us men and for our salvation, came down from heaven, and was incarnate by the Holy Spirit of the virgin Mary, and was made man; and was crucified also for us under Pontius Pilate; He suffered and was buried; and the third day He rose again, according to the Scriptures; and ascended into heaven, and sits on the right hand of the Father; and He shall come again, with glory, to judge the quick and the dead; whose kingdom shall have no end. And I believe in the Holy Ghost, the Lord and Giver of Life; who proceeds from the Father and the Son; who with the Father and the Son together is worshipped and glorified; who spoke by the prophets. And I believe in one holy catholic and apostolic Church. I acknowledge one baptism for the remission of sins; and I look for the resurrection of the dead, and the life of the world to come. Amen.

The Definition of Chalcedon

Therefore, following the holy fathers, we all with one accord teach men to acknowledge one and the same Son, our Lord Jesus Christ, at once complete in Godhead and complete in manhood, truly God and truly man, consisting also of a reasonable soul and body; of one substance with the Father as regards his Godhead, and at the same time of one substance with us as regards his manhood; like us in all respects, apart from sin; as regards his Godhead, begotten of the Father before the ages, but yet as regards his manhood begotten, for us men and for our salvation, of Mary the Virgin, the God-bearer; one and the same Christ, Son, Lord, Only-begotten, recognized in two natures, without confusion, without change, without division, without separation; the distinction of natures being in no way annulled by the union, but rather the characteristics of each nature being preserved and coming together to form one person and subsistence, not as parted or separated into two persons, but one and the same Son and Only-begotten God the Word, Lord Jesus Christ; even as the prophets from earliest times spoke of him, and our Lord Jesus Christ himself taught us, and the creed of the fathers has handed down to us.

The Athanasian Creed

Whosoever will be saved, before all things it is necessary that he hold the catholic faith. Which faith except everyone do keep whole and undefiled, without doubt he shall perish everlastingly. And the catholic faith is this: That we worship one God in Trinity, and Trinity in Unity, neither confounding the persons, nor dividing the substance. For there is one Person of the Father, another of the Son, and another of the Holy Spirit. But the godhead of the Father, of the Son, and of the Holy Spirit, is all one, the glory equal, the majesty co-eternal. Such as the Father is, such is the Son, and such is the Holy Spirit. The Father uncreated, the Son uncreated, and the Holy Spirit uncreated. The Father incomprehensible, the Son incomprehensible, and the Holy Spirit incomprehensible. The Father eternal, the Son eternal, and the Holy Spirit eternal. And yet they are not three eternals, but one Eternal. As also there are not three incomprehensibles, nor three uncreated, but one Uncreated, and one Incomprehensible. So likewise the Father is Almighty, the Son Almighty, and the Holy Spirit Almighty. And yet they are not three almighties, but one Almighty. So the Father is God, the Son is God, and the Holy Spirit is God. And yet they are not three gods, but one God. So likewise the Father is Lord, the Son Lord, and the Holy Spirit Lord. And yet not three lords, but one Lord. For as we are compelled by the Christian verity to acknowledge each Person by Himself to be both God and Lord, so we are also forbidden by the catholic religion to say that there are three gods or three lords. The Father is made of none, neither created, nor begotten. The Son is of the Father alone, not made, nor created, but begotten. The Holy Spirit is of the Father, neither made, nor created, nor begotten, but proceeding. So there is one Father, not three fathers; one Son, not three sons; one Holy Spirit, not three holy spirits. And in the Trinity none is before or after another; none is greater or less than another, but all three Persons are co-eternal together and co-equal. So that in all things, as is aforesaid, the Unity in Trinity and the Trinity in Unity is to be worshipped. He therefore that will be saved must think thus of the Trinity. Furthermore, it is necessary to everlasting salvation that he also believe rightly the Incarnation of our Lord Jesus Christ. For the right faith is, that we believe and confess, that our Lord Jesus Christ, the Son of God, is God and man; God, of the substance of the Father, begotten before the worlds; and man of the substance of his mother, born in the world; perfect God and perfect man, of a rational soul and human flesh subsisting. Equal to the Father, as touching His godhead; and inferior to the Father, as touching His manhood; who, although He is God and man, yet he is not two, but one Christ; one, not by conversion of the godhead into flesh but by taking of the manhood into God; one altogether; not by confusion of substance, but by unity of person. For as the rational soul and flesh is one man, so God and man is one Christ; who suffered for our salvation, descended into hell, rose again the third day from the dead. He ascended into heaven, He sits at the right hand of the Father, God Almighty, from whence He will come to judge the quick and the dead. At His coming all men will rise again with their bodies and shall give account for their own works. And they that have done good shall go into life everlasting; and they that have done evil into everlasting fire.

This is the catholic faith, which except a man believe faithfully, he cannot be saved.

Lesson 3: The Majesty on High (God the Father)

God the Father is the first person of the Trinity. (Deuteronomy 32:6, Psalm 68:5, Isaiah 64:8 Malachi 2:10 Matthew 6:9; 7:11; 23:9, Romans 8:15, 1 Corinthians 8:6 Ephesians 4:6 Hebrews 12:9, 1 Peter 1:17) That is to say that He is first in priority and first in authority. Since all three Persons have existed forever, the Father does not precede either the Son or Holy Spirit as to time or origination. All three have always existed in union with One another. God the Father orders and disposes all things according to His own purposes and grace (Psalm 145:8, 9; 1 Corinthians 8:6), which have God's glory as their end. He is the Creator of all things (Genesis 1:1-31; Ephesians 3:9). God the Father is truly our Redeemer in that He saves from sin all those who come to Him through Jesus Christ. (More on that later)

(We are endeavoring to provide the Classic Orthodox Protestant view of the Person of God):

How do we know about God?
1.   General Revelation
1.   The natural world reveals God (Acts 14:15-17; Rom.1:19-23)
1.   Human Conscience testifies to the existence God (Rom.2:14-16)
1.   Special Revelation
1.   Miracles reveal God.
oGod extends natural laws (Josh.10:12-14 – sun stood still)
oGod supercedes natural laws (2 Kings 6 – axehead floated)
1.   Fulfilled prophecy reveals God.
oO.T. (Is.43:28-45; Ezra 1:1-4 – Cyrus predicted)
oN.T. (Micah 5:2; Matt.2:1 – birthplace of Christ)
1.   Jesus Christ Himself reveals God. (Heb.1:1; John 1:18)
1.   Scripture as a whole reveals God.

Can we prove God's existence?
1.   The Bible assumes God's existence rather than attempting to prove it (Gen.1:1).
1.   The natural world demands God's existence (Ps.19; Is.40:26; Acts 14:17; Rom.1:19).
1.   Argument from Cosmology – How could there be anything if there wasn't a Cause (God) who was Uncaused (Romans 1:20)? Quoting Dr. Sproul, "IF THERE EVER WAS A TIME WHEN ABSOLUTELY NOTHING EXISTED, ALL THERE COULD POSSIBLY BE NOW IS NOTHING."
1.   Argument from Teleology – The mathematical precision and obvious intelligence in Nature demands a designer of infinitely superior intellect. (God - Psalm 19:1-6)?
1.   Moral argument –If there is no one to give a Law, who then is the arbiter of right and wrong? (God – Romans 2:14,15; James 4:12)?

1.   Ontological argument – Where do people get the idea of a Perfect Being (God) except from God Himself (Act 17:27; Romans 1:19)? Can we describe or explain God? How do we do so? God has many perfect characteristics (attributes). Attributes are the characteristics that define the essence of the Godhead

oIncommunicable attributes (characteristics belonging only to God).

oSelf-existence (Exodus 3:14, John 5:26).

oImmutability (Psalm 102:25-27; Ex.3:14; James 1:17) – God does not change His essence or plan. He can never be wiser, more holy, more just, more merciful, more truthful. Neither can God be any less of any of those as any change would make Him less than God. His plans and His purposes never change (Ps 33:11)

oInfinity (Psalm 147:5, 1 Kings 8:27, Psalm 145:3, Ephesians 3:8, Revelation 19:6, Psalm 113:4-6, Revelation 1:8, Isaiah 40:28, Jeremiah 23:24, 2 Chronicles 2:6, 2 Chronicles 6:18, 1 Timothy 6:16, Romans 11:33

oEternality – Infinite in time (Psalm 90:2)

oOmnipresence – Infinite in space (Ps.139:7-11) Present everywhere at once (Jeremiah 23:23-24) Yet transcends His creation and as such He is always able to help us, His creatures (Ps 46:1, Matt 28:20) He is inescapable (Ps 139:7-10, 17)

oHoliness – The absence of evil and presence of purity (Lev.11:44; John 17:11; 1 John 1:5)

oHoly: God is separate from and exalted above all of His creatures God is free from all defilement, absolutely pure) Isaiah 6:3. Holiness is the foremost attribute of God – the attribute by which He especially wants to be known. God's Throne is established upon His holiness, thereby regulating His love, power, and will

By God's holiness we know:
1.   There is great chasm between God and the sinner (Is 59:1-2 Habakkuk 1:13)
1.   Man must approach God through the merits of another if he is to be able to approach Him at all because man does not possess nor can he ever acquire the sinlessness necessary for access to God (Rom 5:1-2, 6-8, Ephesians 2:1-9, 18, Hebrews 10:19-20)
1.   We must approach God with humility, awe and reverence (Hebrews 12:28)

God is Righteous and just
God has instituted a moral government in the world, imposed just laws on His creatures, and attached sanctions for disobedience. God cannot make a law, establish a penalty, and then not follow through when the law is disobeyed. Punishment must be given, either personally or vicariously. The purpose of punishment is to maintain justice (Is 53:10, Psalm 145:17)

God has communicable attributes (characteristics found in a limited degree in man). God's communicable attributes are:

1. Intellect
1. Omniscience – God knows all things actual and potential. The Bible does not explain this but does assume it as fact (Ps.139:16; Matt. 11:21).
1. All-wise – God acts upon His knowledge to always do what is infinitely best (Rom.11:33-36).

Attributes of Emotion

oGod is Love – God is incomprehensibly active for our good (1 John 4:8).
oMercy – concern, compassion (James 5:11)
oLong suffering – self-restrained when provoked (2 Peter 3:9,15)
oGod is just – God is perfectly righteous and exact in His dealings with man (Ps.19:9).

God's most recognizable attribute is grace.

1. Grace- (Definition and comments from Wayne Kinde.) A special characteristic of God involving many of His major loving characteristics
1. OT uses chesed and chen. There are multiple different ways that these are translated in the OT. Examples: love, mercy, compassion, tenderheartedness, kindness, grace, favor, etc.

For further study

1. Septuagint (Greek OT/LXX) renderings of charis and what Hebrew words were used for this very generic and bland Greek word. This will, again, show a huge diversity in the usage (FAR beyond, "unmerited favor").
1. In the Hellenistic period (maybe best between 200BC-0BC). How was it used extensively prior the the NT writings. There you will see quite again a wide variety of usages, from love, mercy, peace, compassion, and favor.
1. In the NT, what is the overacrching sense of the word based on the above and each context.

Looking at the historical data from above, I conclude that the word "grace" demonstrates a major character of the Trinity regarding many of the major loving characteristics. Thus, it is by this grace (His amazing love, compassion, mercy, tenderheartedness, etc.) that we are saved (Eph 2:8).

Another of my teachers puts it this way: Grace is God's goodness manifested toward the guilty undeserving, to those deserving His justice instead

Additional Communicable Attributes of God

1. Will
1. Omnipotence (Job 42:2) God is able to do anything He wills. He will not do anything against His nature (sin) and He cannot do anything that is logically self-contradictory. Because God can only do what is in harmony with His nature He cannot

    lie (Titus 1:2)
    repent from evil (Numbers 23:19)
    deny Himself (2 Tim 2:13)

be tempted to sin (James 1:13)

In other words, in congruence with His nature, God can do anything that is logically possible and cannot do anything that is logically impossible, such as those mentioned above.

Sovereignty (2 Chronicles 29:11,12) As the only absolute and omnipotent ruler in the universe, He is sovereign in creation, providence, and redemption (Psalm 103:19; Romans 11:36). He has decreed for His own glory all things that come to pass (Ephesians 1:11). He continually upholds, directs, and governs all creatures and events (1Chronicles 29:11). In His sovereignty, He is neither author nor approver of sin (Habakkuk 1:13), nor does He abridge the accountability of moral, intelligent creatures (1 Peter 1:17). He has graciously chosen from eternity past those whom He would have as His own (Ephesians 1:4-6) and in that choosing has sovereignly decreed their salvation.

God as Father

God, as Father, reigns with providential care over His universe, His creatures, and human history according to the purposes of His grace. His fatherhood involves both His position within the Trinity and His relationship with mankind.

As Creator He is Father to all men (Ephesians 4:6),

Spiritual Father only to believers (Romans 8:14; 2 Corinthians 6:18).

He adopts as His own all those who come to Him; and He becomes, upon adoption, Father to His own (John 1:12; Romans 8:15; Galatians 4:5; Hebrews 12:5-9).

Lesson 4: The Divine Son

The earliest Creeds/Statements of Faith of the Church teach a belief in the Trinity. In this lesson, we are looking at the 2nd Person of the Trinity. Prior to the Incarnation, His identity was shrouded in the mystery of the Godhead. Since the Incarnation, we now refer to Him by the Name by which He was known on Earth, the Lord Jesus Christ.

Jesus Christ, the second person of the Trinity, possesses all the attributes of the Godhead, and in/because of these He is coequal, consubstantial, and coeternal with the Father (John 10:30; 14:9). As the 2nd Person of the Godhead, Jesus shares these attributes with His Father:

1.   He is eternal (John 1:1-3 with 1 John 1:1-4, John 1:15, John 8:58, John 17:5, 24, Hebrews 1:11)
1.   He is omnipresent (John 3:13, Matthew 18:20, Ephesians 1:23)
1.   He is omniscient (John 16:30, John 21:17, Colossians 2:3, John 4:29, Luke 6:8)
1.   He is omnipotent (John 5:19, Hebrews 1:2-3, Matthew 28:18)
1.   He is immutable (Hebrews 1:12, Hebrews 13:8)
1.   Creator and Sustainer (John 1:3, Colossians 1:15-17, Hebrews 1:3, 10 Psalm 33:6)
1.   Jesus Christ has the prerogatives of God (Matthew 9:2, 6; Luke 7:47- John 5:25-29 John 6:39, John 11:25-26 John 5:22)
Further, Jesus names Himself as God and explains I AM in John's Gospel (Exodus 3:14). Jesus uses "I AM" 7 times, declaring Himself to be
1.   the Bread of Life (6:35, 41)
1.   the Light of the world (8:12)
1.   the Good Shepherd (10:11, 14)
1.   the Door (10:7, 9)
1.   the Way the Truth and the Life (14:6)
1.   the Resurrection and the Life (11:25-26)
1.   the True Vine (15:1)
There is a question of Sonship that has reared its ugly head in recent days, so we will address that by way of our friends at Got Questions Ministries
Eternal Sonship (gotquestions.org)
"The doctrine of eternal Sonship simply affirms that the second Person of the triune Godhead has eternally existed as the Son. In other words, there was never a time when He was not the Son of God, and there has always been a Father/Son relationship within the Godhead. This doctrine recognizes that the idea of Sonship is not merely a title or role that Christ assumed at some specific point in history, but that it is the essential identity of the second Person of the Godhead. According to this doctrine, Christ is and always has been the Son of God.
Yes, the eternal Sonship is biblical and is a view that is widely held among Christians and has been throughout church history. It is important, however, to remember when discussing the doctrine of eternal Sonship that there are evangelical Christians on both sides of this debate. This is not to say that this is not an important doctrine, because it is; it simply acknowledges the fact that there are orthodox or evangelical Christians that hold or have held both views. Those that deny the doctrine of eternal Sonship are not denying the triune nature of God or the deity or eternality of Christ, and those that embrace the eternal Sonship of Christ are not inferring that Jesus Christ was anything less than fully God.
Throughout church history the doctrine of eternal Sonship has been widely held, with most Christians believing that Jesus existed as God's eternal Son before creation. It is affirmed in the Nicene Creed (325 A.D.) which states:

"We believe in one God, the Father, the Almighty, maker of heaven and earth, of all that is, seen and unseen. We believe in one Lord, Jesus Christ, the only Son of God, eternally begotten of the Father, God from God, Light from Light, true God from true God, begotten, not made, of one Being with the Father. Through him all things were made. For us and for our salvation he came down from heaven: by the power of the Holy Spirit he became incarnate from the Virgin Mary, and was made man. For our sake he was crucified under Pontius Pilate; he suffered death and was buried. On the third day he rose again in accordance with the Scriptures; he ascended into heaven and is seated at the right hand of the Father. He will come again in glory to judge the living and the dead, and his kingdom will have no end." It was also later reaffirmed in the fifth century in the Athanasian Creed.

There is considerable biblical evidence to support the eternal Sonship of Christ. First of all, there are many passages that clearly identify that it was "the Son" who created all things (Colossians 1:13-16; Hebrews 1:2), thereby strongly implying that Christ was the Son of God at the time of creation. When one considers these passages, it seems clear that the most normal and natural meaning of the passages is that at the time of creation Jesus was the Son of God, the second Person of the Triune Godhead, thus supporting the doctrine of eternal Sonship.

Second, there are numerous verses that speak of God the Father sending the Son into the world to redeem sinful man (John 20:21; Galatians 4:4; 1 John 4:14; 1 John 4:10) and giving His Son as a sacrifice for sin (John 3:16). Clearly implied in all the passages that deal with the Father sending/giving the Son is the fact that He was the Son before He was sent into the world. This is even more clearly seen in Galatians 4:4-6, where the term "sent forth" is used both of the Son and the Spirit. Just as the Holy Spirit did not become the Holy Spirit when He was sent to empower the believers at Pentecost, neither did the Son become the Son at the moment of His incarnation. All three Persons of the Triune Godhead have existed for all eternity, and their names reveal who they are, not simply what their title or function is.

Third, 1 John 3:8 speaks of the appearance or manifestation of the Son of God: "the one who practices sin is of the devil; for the devil has sinned from the beginning. The Son of God appeared for this purpose, that He might destroy the works of the devil." The verb "to make manifest" or "appeared" means to make visible or to bring to light something that was previously hidden. The idea communicated in this verse is not that the second Person of the trinity became the Son of God, but that the already existing Son of God was made manifest or appeared in order to fulfill God's predetermined purpose. This idea is also seen in other verses such as John 11:27 and 1 John 5:20.

Fourth, Hebrews 13:8 teaches that "Jesus Christ is the same yesterday and today, yes and forever." This verse, again, seems to support the doctrine of eternal Sonship. The fact that Jesus' divine nature is unchanging would seem to indicate that He was always the Son of God because that is an essential part of His Person. At the incarnation Jesus took on human flesh, but His divine nature did not change, nor did His relationship with the Father. This same truth is also implied in John 20:31, where we see John's purpose in writing his gospel was so that we might "believe that Jesus is the Christ, the Son of God; and that believing you may have life in His name." It does not say that He became the Son of God but that He is the Son of God. The fact that Jesus was and is the Son of God is an essential aspect of Who He is and His work in redemption.

Finally, one of the strongest evidences for the eternal Sonship of Christ is the triune nature of God and the eternal relationship that exists among the Father, Son, and Holy Spirit. Particularly important is the unique Father/Son relationship that can only be understood from the aspect of Christ's eternal Sonship. This relationship is key to understanding the full measure of God's love for those whom He redeems through the blood of Christ. The fact that God the Father took His Son, the very Son He loved from before the foundation of the world, and sent Him to be a sacrifice for our sins is an amazing act of grace and love that is best understood from the doctrine of eternal Sonship.

One verse that speaks of the eternal relationship between the Father and Son is John 16:28. "I came forth from the Father, and have come into the world; I am leaving the world again, and going to the Father." Implied in this verse is again the fact that the Father/Son relationship between God the Father and God the Son is one that always has and always will exist. At His incarnation the Son "came from the Father" in the same sense as upon His resurrection He returned "to the Father." Implied in this verse is the fact that if Jesus was the Son after the resurrection, then He was also the Son prior to His incarnation. Other verses that support the eternal Sonship of Christ would include John 17:5 and John 17:24, which speak of the Father's love for the Son from "before the foundation of the world."

After one considers the many arguments for the doctrine of eternal Sonship, it should become clear that this is indeed a biblical doctrine that finds much support in Scripture. However, that is not to imply that arguments cannot be made against the doctrine as well, or that all Christians will agree to this doctrine. While it has been the view of the majority of Christian commentators throughout history, there have been several prominent Christians on the other side of the issue as well."

The term, "son of God," occurs more than 40 times in the Bible, all of them in the New Testament. The phrase is found in the KJV in Daniel 3:25, but the Hebrew word of God is actually in the plural so it should read, "son of the gods." So, what do we find when we examine the phrase in the New Testament? The New Testament declares:

o**Jesus Christ is the Son of God, (Matthew 26:63, Mark 1:1, John 20:31, Heb. 4:14).**

oUnclean spirits would fall down before Jesus and say, "You are the Son of God," (Mark 3:11).

o" . . . the holy offspring shall be called the Son of God," (Luke 1:35).

oAdam is said to be the son of God (Luke 3:38).

oThose who hear the voice of the Son of God shall live (John 5:25).

oPaul had faith in the Son of God (Galatians 2:20).

oSon of God has no beginning or end (Hebrews 7:3).

oThe Son of God appeared to destroy the works of the devil (1 John 3:8).

oBelieve in the Son of God so that you may have eternal life (1 John 5:13).

We can see that the term refers to the majesty, position, and power of Jesus who is holy (Luke 1:35), associated with salvation (John 5:25) and that we are to have faith in the Son of God (Galatians 2:20) so as to have eternal life (1 John 5:13) and that He has no beginning or end (Hebrews 7:3). The only exception to this flow of exultation is Luke 3:38 when it says Adam was the "Son of God," but here the context is a genealogy, and we know that Adam was the first man created by God.

Furthermore, in reference to Jesus, the term, "Son of God," does not mean that Jesus is the literal offspring of God as if God had some form of sexual relations with Mary to produce Jesus. God is spirit (John 4:24), and spirit does not have flesh and bones (Luke 24:39), so God the Father is not the literal father of Jesus.

Jesus can be both God and the Son of God because the terms don't mean the same thing. When we say that Jesus is God (John 1:1, 14, Colossians 2:9, Hebrews 1:8), we are saying that Jesus possesses the divine nature (as well as a human nature; for further study research the term hypostatic union. The short explanation is that, in hypostatic union, the two natures as the Divine Son and as Man exist simultaneously in a single person). But the term, "Son of God," does not mean that Jesus is not God. Think about it. If the term, "Son of God," meant that Jesus is not God, then does the term, "Son of Man," mean that Jesus is not a man? Of course not. Likewise, if the term, "Son of Man," means that Jesus is a man, then does it not imply that when it says that Jesus is the "Son of God," that He is God? We ought not look at the ancient words found in Scripture and judge them by modern thinking.

"For this reason therefore the Jews were seeking all the more to kill Him, because He not only was breaking the Sabbath, but also was calling God His own Father, making Himself equal with God," (John 5:18).

As you can see in this verse, Jesus was calling God His own Father, making Himself equal to God. Therefore, the term, Son of God, is a designation of the equality with God when it is a reference to Christ.

Those that deny the doctrine of eternal Sonship would instead hold to a view that is often referred to as the Incarnational Sonship, which teaches that while Christ preexisted, He was not always the Son of God. Those that hold this view believe Christ became the Son of God at some point in history, with the most common view being that Christ became the Son at His incarnation.

However, there are others who believe Christ did not become the Son until sometime after His incarnation, such as at His baptism, His resurrection, or His exaltation. It is important to realize that those who deny the eternal Sonship of Christ still recognize and affirm His deity and His eternality. Those who hold this view see the Sonship of Christ as not being an essential part of Who He is, but instead see it as simply being a role or a title or function that Christ assumed at His incarnation. They also teach that the Father became the Father at the time of the incarnation. Throughout history many conservative Christians have denied the doctrine of eternal Sonship. Some examples would include Ralph Wardlaw, Adam Clarke, Albert Barnes, Finis J. Dake, Walter Martin, and, at one time, John MacArthur. It is important to note, however, that several years ago John MacArthur changed his position on this doctrine and he now affirms the doctrine of eternal Sonship.

One of the verses commonly used to support Incarnational Sonship is Hebrews 1:5, which appears to speak of God the Father's begetting of God the Son as an event that takes place at a specific point in time: "Thou art My Son, Today I have begotten Thee. And again. I will be a Father to Him. And He shall be a Son to Me." Those who hold to the doctrine of incarnational Sonship point out two important aspects of this verse. 1—that "begetting" normally speaks of a person's origin, and 2—that a Son is normally subordinate to his father. They reject the doctrine of eternal Sonship in an attempt to preserve the perfect equality and eternality of the Persons of the Triune Godhead. In order to do so, they must conclude that "Son" is simply a title or function that Christ took on at His incarnation and that "Sonship" refers to the voluntary submission that Christ took to the Father at His incarnation (Philippians 2:5-8; John 5:19).

Some of the problems with the Incarnational Sonship of Christ are that this teaching confuses or destroys the internal relationships that exist within the Trinity, because if the Son is not eternally begotten by the Father, then neither did the Spirit eternally proceed from the Father through the Son. Also, if there is no Son prior to the incarnation, then there is no Father either; and yet throughout the Old Testament we see God being referred to as the Father of Israel. Instead of having a triune God eternally existing in three distinct Persons with three distinct names, Father, Son, and Holy Spirit, those who hold to the doctrine of incarnational Sonship end up with a nameless Trinity prior to the incarnation, and we would be forced to say that God has chosen not to reveal Himself as He truly is, but only as He was to become. In other words, instead of actually revealing who He is, the Triune God instead chose to reveal Himself by the titles He would assume or the roles that He would take on and not who He really is. This is dangerously close to modalism and could easily lead to false teachings about the nature of God. One of the weaknesses of the doctrine of incarnational Sonship is that the basic relationships existing among the members of the Trinity are confused and diminished. Taken to its logical conclusion, denying the eternal Sonship of Christ reduces the Trinity from the relationship of Father, Son, and Holy Spirit to simply Number One, Number Two and Number Three Persons—with the numbers themselves being an arbitrary designation, destroying the God-given order and relationship that exists among the Persons of the Trinity.

God the Father created "the heavens and the earth and all that is in them" according to His own will, through His Son, Jesus Christ, by whom all things continue in existence and in operations (John 1:3; Colossians 1:15-17; Hebrews 1:2).

The 2nd Person of the Trinity as the God-man

In the incarnation (God becoming man) Christ surrendered/laid aside His prerogatives as God but nothing of the divine essence, either in degree or kind, instead subordinating Himself to the will of God the Father and accepting the limitations of humanity. In His incarnation, the eternally existing second person of the Trinity accepted all the essential characteristics of humanity and so became the God-man (Philippians 2:5-8; Colossians 2:9).

Jesus Christ represents, perfectly, humanity and deity in indivisible oneness (Micah 5:2; John 5:23; 14:9, 10; Colossians 2:9).

The Definition of the Council of Chalcedon (451 A.D) explains further... Therefore, following the holy fathers, we all with one accord teach men to acknowledge one and the same Son, our Lord Jesus Christ, at once complete in Godhead and complete in manhood, truly God and truly man, consisting also of a reasonable soul and body; of one substance with the Father as regards his Godhead, and at the same time of one substance with us as regards his manhood; like us in all respects, apart from sin; as regards his Godhead, begotten of the Father before the ages, but yet as regards his manhood begotten, for us men and for our salvation, of Mary the Virgin, the God-bearer; one and the same Christ, Son, Lord, Only-begotten, recognized in two natures, without confusion, without change, without division, without separation; the distinction of natures being in no way annulled by the union, but rather the characteristics of each nature being preserved and coming together to form one person and subsistence, not as parted or separated into two persons, but one and the same Son and Only-begotten God the Word, Lord Jesus Christ; even as the prophets from earliest times spoke of him, and our Lord Jesus Christ himself taught us, and the creed of the fathers has handed down to us.

The Scriptures teach:

In His Incarnation, the Lord Jesus Christ was virgin born (Isaiah 7:14; Matthew 1:23, 25; Luke 1:26-35); that He was God incarnate (John 1:1, 14); and that the purpose of the incarnation was to reveal God, redeem men, and rule over God's kingdom (Psalms 2:7-9; Isaiah 9:6; John 1:29; Philippians 2:9-11; Hebrew 7:25, 26; 1Peter 1:18, 19).

There is some controversy surrounding Isaiah 7:14 and I want to address that, here. Our friends on the NASB and Amplified Bible Translation Committee (same committee for both) provide us the following...

"Isaiah 7:14 This prophecy of the *virgin* is declared in Matt 1:22, 23 to be fulfilled in the birth of Jesus. There has been a great deal of discussion over the Hebrew word found here for *virgin* (*almah*) and the word that Matthew uses (*parthenos*). The latter refers unambiguously to a virgin, while the former (*almah*) has been said to refer to a young woman, in contrast to the Hebrew word *bethulah*, which is the equivalent of the Gr *parthenos*. It has also been noted that the Septuagint, the Greek translation of the Hebrew OT, has *parthenos* here for *almah*, and that Matt 1:23 is taken from the Septuagint. Some have wondered why the Septuagint translators used the more specific word *parthenos*. It is fair to say that this question is the result of oversimplifying the vocabulary and misinterpreting the distinctions. The Hebrew words *almah* and *bethulah* can actually refer to the same kind of woman; *almah* is a youthful woman of marriageable age, one who has not yet had her first child, while *bethulah* is one who has not been touched in an intimate way. Furthermore, in the present context it would be unthinkable to infer that the woman might have had sexual relations outside of marriage. So the well-known translation of "young woman" for *almah*, while technically not incorrect, can be viewed as too ambiguous for the Hebrew word and the context. *Parthenos* was an appropriate choice in the Greek. Another word, *kore* (for "girl") could have been used, but it has a wider range of meaning than the Heb *almah* (Mark uses a related word, *korasion*, to translate Jesus' Aramaic word *talitha*). It should also be acknowledged from a theological perspective that when Matthew cites the verse with *parthenos*, he thereby authenticates it as inspired."

In the incarnation, the second person of the Trinity laid aside His right to the full prerogatives of coexistence with God, assumed the place of a Son, and took on an existence appropriate to a servant while never divesting Himself of His divine attributes (Philippians 2:5-8).

Why did God the Son become man? Why did He subject Himself to His creatures and allow Himself to be humiliated?
oto fulfill God's promises (Isaiah 9:6, Isaiah 7:14, Micah 5:2, Daniel 9:26)
oto reveal the Father to man
oGod had been revealed as Creator and Lord now He is revealed to be Father, completing the revelation
oto become a faithful High Priest
oa sinless High Priest to represent man (Hebrews 2:17-18, Hebrews 5:1-3, Hebrews 7:25-27)

oto put away/put an end to sin (Hebrews 9:26, Mark 10:45, 1 John 3:5, Leviticus 16:20-22, John 1:29, Isaiah 53:6, 2 Corinthians 5:21)
oto destroy the works of Satan (1 John 3:8, Hebrews 2:14-15, John 12:31)
oto give us an example of holy living (1 Peter 2:21, 1 John 2:6 {saved then follow})

There are some awe commanding events with the incarnation of God the Son
oHe emptied Himself
oThe humiliation of Christ began in His attitude (Phil 2:6), showing us the necessity of an attitude of humility
oHis divine glory was veiled, but not surrendered (Matt 17:1)
oHe voluntarily restricted His attributes of Deity in keeping with His purpose to live among men and all their limitations i.e. He remained "in the form of God" as He accepted also the nature of a servant
oHe was made in the likeness of man
oFlesh that was subject to weakness, pain, temptation, incredible limitations so that God could dwell among us (John 1:14)
obut He did not take on man's sinful nature (Rom 8:3)
oHe did not exchange natures, He took an additional nature

During His time on Earth, The Lord Jesus Christ accomplished our redemption through the shedding of His blood and sacrificial death on the cross and that His death was voluntary, vicarious, substitutionary, propitiatory, and redemptive (John 10:15; Romans 3:24, 25; 5:8; 1Peter 2:24). In the future, we will look at both of the major views on the Atonement, the traditional Reformed view known as Penal Substitutionary Atonement, and view known as Christus Victor. The two are often seen, needlessly, as being in opposition to each other. Both, however, are accurate portrayals of the Atonement and neither should be considered as being more accurate than the other.

On the basis of the efficacy of the death of our Lord Jesus Christ, the believing sinner is freed from the punishment, the penalty, the power, and one day the very presence of sin; and that he is declared righteous, given eternal life, and adopted into the family of God (Romans 3:25; 5:8, 9; 2Corinthians 5:14, 15; 1Peter 2:24; 3:18). {This is the Penal Substitutionary Atonement}
Our justification is made sure by His literal, physical resurrection from the dead and the fact that He is now ascended to the right hand of the Father, where He mediates as our Advocate and High-Priest (Matthew 28:6; Luke 24:38, 39; Acts 2:30, 31; Romans 4:25; 8:34; Hebrews 7:25; 9:24; 1 John 2:1). In the resurrection of Jesus Christ from the grave, God confirmed the deity of His Son and gave proof that God has accepted the atoning work of Christ on the cross. Jesus' bodily resurrection is also the guarantee of a future resurrection life for all believers (John 5:26-29; 14:19; Romans 4:25; 6:5-10; 1 Corinthians 15:20, 23).

In the Resurrection to come, Jesus Christ will return to receive the church, which is His body, unto Himself at the Rapture and, after the Tribulation, returning with His church in glory, will establish His millennial kingdom on earth (Acts 1:9-11; 1 Thessalonians 4:13-18; Revelation 20).

The Lord Jesus Christ is the one through whom God will judge all mankind (John 5:22, 23):

oBelievers (1 Corinthians 3:10-15; 2 Corinthians 5:10);

oLiving inhabitants of the earth at His glorious return (Matthew 25:31-46); and

oUnbelieving dead at the Great White Throne (Revelation 20:11-15).

As the mediator between God and man (1 Timothy 2:5), the head of His body the church (Ephesians 1:22; 5:23; Colossians 1:18), and the coming universal King who will reign on the throne of David (Isaiah 9:6, 7; Ezekiel 37:24-28; Luke 1:31-33), He is the final judge of all who fail to place their trust in Him as Lord and Savior (Matthew 25:14-46; Acts 17:30, 31).

Lesson 5: The Holy Spirit

The Holy Spirit is a Person

In Greek, personal pronouns are used - He, Him, etc. Greek (parakletos) - "One called alongside to help", Helper, Comforter, Counselor.

The Holy Spirit possesses attributes of personhood

Intellect. Romans 8:26: ... the Spirit Himself makes intercession for us with groanings which cannot be uttered. Intercession requires intellect.

Emotions. Ephesians 4:30: And do not grieve the Holy Spirit of God.

A Will. Luke 2:26: And it had been revealed unto him by the Holy Spirit, that he should not see death, before he had seen the Lord's Messiah. To actively reveal something is an act of the will.

The Holy Spirit does things only a Person can do:

oteaches and helps us to remember John 14:26

ocalls men to service (He speaks) Acts 13:2

oconvicts us of sin John 16:8

oleads Romans 8:13,14

oauthors 2 Peter 1:19-21

being a Person, He can be affected by our actions or attitudes.

1. We can lie to Him (Acts 5:1-3)
1. We can grieve Him (Ephesians 4:30)
1. We can quench Him (1 Thessalonians 5:19)
1. We can insult Him (Hebrews 10:29)
1. We can resist Him (Acts 7:51)
1. We can blaspheme Him (Mark 3:28-29)
1. We are convicted by Him (John 16:7-11)

The Holy Spirit is God Himself

In possessing the same essential qualities that Jesus does, He possesses all of the attributes of God:

1. Omnipresent (Psalms 139:7-10)
1. Omnipotent (Luke 1:35)
1. Omniscient (John 14:26; 16:12-13 1 Corinthians 2:10-11)
1. Eternal (Hebrews 9:14)
1. Holy (Romans 1:4)
1. Creator (Genesis 1:2, Job 33:4; Ps 104:30)
1. He is called God (Acts 5:3-4, 2 Corinthians 3:3, 17)
1. He fills (Acts 4:8, Ephesians 5:18)
1. He empowers/comes upon {epi} (Rom 8:13, Gal 5:17, Zechariah 4:6 Acts 1:8)
1. He teaches (John 14:26, John 16:13, Nehemiah 9:20 1 John 2:27)
1. He edifies (Acts 9:31)

The Holy Spirit never calls attention to Himself. He is ever present to glorify and testify to the Lord Jesus Christ. This is His good pleasure and the the outworking of His Divine will. It pleases the Holy Spirit to glorify the Son and in so doing to glorify the Father.

John 16:13-14: However, when He, the Spirit of Truth, has come, He will guide you into all truth. For He shall not speak of Himself, but whatever He hears, He shall speak. And He will announce to you things to come. He will glorify Me, for He will receive of Mine and will announce it to you.

The Spirit of God actively convicts the world of sin, righteousness and judgment

John 16:8: And when that One comes, He will convict the world concerning sin, and concerning righteousness, and concerning judgment.

He regenerates the believers

John 3:6-7: That which is born of the flesh is flesh, and that which is born of the Spirit is spirit. Do not marvel that I said to you, "You must be born again."

The Holy Ghost seals believers unto the day of redemption

Ephesians 4:30: And do not grieve the Holy Spirit of God, by whom you are sealed until the day of redemption.

The Holy Spirit sanctifies believers

Galatians 5:16: I say, then, walk in the Spirit and you shall not fulfill the lusts of flesh.

At the moment of salvation, each believer is baptized into the Holy Spirit

1 Corinthians 12:13: For also by one Spirit we are all baptized into one body, whether Jews or Greeks, whether bond or free, even all were made to drink into one Spirit.

To quote Dr. Stanley, at the moment of your salvation, you got all of the Holy Spirit that you are ever going to get.

At the moment of salvation, the believer is permanently indwelt by the Spirit.

John 14:16-17: And I will pray the Father, and He shall give you another Comforter, so that He may be with you forever, the Spirit of Truth, whom the world cannot receive because it does not see Him nor know Him. But you know Him, for He dwells with you and shall be in you.

The Holy Spirit gives gifts to the believer for building up the church

1 Corinthians 12:7-8: And to each hath been given the manifestation of the Spirit for profit; for to one through the Spirit hath been given a word of wisdom, and to another a word of knowledge, according to the same Spirit.

What about the charismata (grace gifts/gifts of the Spirit)?

The Gift of the Spirit is the Holy Spirit himself, and He is to be desired more than the Grace Gifts, which He in His wise counsel bestows upon individual members of the Church to enable them properly to fulfill their function as members of the body of Christ. The gifts of the Spirit, although not always identifiable with natural abilities, function through them for the edification of the whole Church. These gifts are to be exercised in love under the administration of the Lord of the Church, not through human volition. The relative value of the gifts of the Spirit is to be tested by their usefulness in the Church and not by the ecstasy produced in the ones receiving them. The purpose of spiritual gifts is to edify the whole Church not the individual.

The Problem (especially for Charismatics) with seeking the sign gifts is a lack of knowledge of the Person of the Holy Spirit and the proper exercise of His gifts.

The gifts are ALWAYS to focus the believer on Jesus never to focus on the believer himself. He gifts us by His sovereign will...and takes into account our unique personalities. Gifts complement each other, never compete with each other

The Cessation of the Sign Gifts (Are the Sign Gifts for Today)

The biblical record shows that miracles occurred during particular periods for the specific purpose of authenticating a new message from God.

oMoses was enabled to perform miracles to authenticate his ministry before Pharaoh (Exodus 4:1-8).

oElijah was given miracles to authenticate his ministry before Ahab (1 Kings 17:1; 18:24).

oThe apostles were given miracles to authenticate their ministry before Israel (Acts 4:10, 16).

oJesus' ministry was also marked by miracles, which the Apostle John calls "signs" (John 2:11). John's point is that the miracles were proofs of the authenticity of Jesus' message.

After Jesus' resurrection, as the Church was being established and the New Testament was being written, the apostles demonstrated "signs" such as tongues and the power to heal. "Tongues are for a sign, not to them that believe, but to them that believe not" (1 Corinthians 14:22), a verse that plainly says the gift was never intended to edify the church.

As the "Gift of Tongues" seems to be the most common gift sought today, we will focus on it for our arguments

Evidence from Scripture

Is there biblical or theological evidence that tongues have ceased? Yes.

First, the gift of tongues was a miraculous, revelatory gift, and the age of miracles and, especially, revelation ended with the apostles. The last recorded miracles in the New Testament occurred around A.D. 58, with the healings on the island of Malta (Acts 28:7-10). From A.D. 58 to 96, when John finished the book of Revelation, no miracle is recorded. Miracle gifts like tongues and healing are mentioned only in 1 Corinthians, an early epistle and possibly one of the first penned by the Apostle Paul. Two later epistles, Ephesians and Romans, both discuss gifts of the Spirit at length—but no mention is made of the miraculous gifts.

By that time miracles were already looked on as something in the past (Hebrews 2:3-4). Apostolic authority and the apostolic message needed no further confirmation. Before the first century ended, the entire New Testament had been written and was circulating through the churches.

John MacArthur makes an excellent point and adds a powerful question:

Charismatic believers insist that none of the gifts have ceased and non-charismatics insist that tongues have already ceased. Who is right and what is the implication?

By the time the apostolic age ended with the death of the Apostle John, the signs that identified the apostles had already become moot (2 Corinthians 12:12).

Secondly, tongues were intended as a sign to unbelieving Israel (1 Corinthians 14:21-22; Isaiah 28:11-12). They signified that God had begun a new work that encompassed the Gentiles. The Lord would now speak to all nations in all languages. The barriers were down. And so the gift of languages symbolized not only the curse of God on a disobedient nation, but also the blessing of God on the whole world. (Here, in a sense, God reversed, or rather superceded, for a time, what He did at the Tower of Babel by confusing humanity's languages.)

Tongues were therefore a sign of transition between the Old and New Covenants. With the establishment of the church, a new day had dawned for the people of God. God would speak in all languages. But once the period of transition was past, the sign would no longer be necessary.

Third, the gift of tongues was inferior to other gifts. It was given primarily as a sign (1 Corinthians 14:22) and was also easily misused to edify self (1 Corinthians 14:4). Case in point, the number of people who foolishly claim that all believers should expect this gift, or the even more dangerous teaching that one cannot truly be saved if He does not speak in tongues. The church meets for the edification of the body, not self-gratification or personal experience-seeking. Therefore, tongues had limited usefulness in the church, and so it was never intended to be a permanent gift.

Evidence from History

The evidence of history indicates that tongues have ceased. It is significant that tongues are mentioned only in the earliest books of the New Testament. Paul wrote at least twelve epistles after 1 Corinthians and never mentioned tongues again. Peter never mentioned tongues; James never mentioned tongues; John never mentioned tongues; neither did Jude. Tongues appeared only briefly in Acts and 1 Corinthians as the new message of the gospel was being spread. But once the church was established, tongues were gone. They stopped. The later books of the New Testament do not mention tongues again, and neither did anyone in the post-apostolic age.

Chrysostom and Augustine—the greatest theologians of the eastern and western churches—considered tongues obsolete. Writing in the fourth century, Chrysostom stated categorically that tongues had ceased by his time and described the gift as an obscure practice. Augustine referred to tongues as a sign that was adapted to the apostolic age. In fact, during the first five hundred years of the church, the only people who claimed to have spoken in tongues were followers of Montanus, who was branded as a heretic.

The Apostle Paul predicted that the gift of tongues would cease (1 Corinthians 13:8). To repeat and reinforce the point, here are six proofs {gotquestions.org} that it has already ceased:

1) The apostles, through whom tongues came, were unique in the history of the church. Once their ministry was accomplished, the need for authenticating signs ceased to exist.

2) The miracle (or sign) gifts are only mentioned in the earliest epistles, such as 1 Corinthians. Later books, such as Ephesians and Romans, contain detailed passages on the gifts of the Spirit, but the miracle gifts are not mentioned, although Romans does mention the gift of prophecy. The Greek word translated "prophecy" means "speaking forth" and does not necessarily include prediction of the future.

3) The gift of tongues was a sign to unbelieving Israel that God's salvation was now available to other nations. See 1 Corinthians 14:21-22 and Isaiah 28:11-12.

4) Tongues was an inferior gift to prophecy (preaching). Preaching the Word of God edifies (builds up/trains/molds) believers, whereas tongues does not.

Believers are told to seek prophesying over speaking in tongues (1 Corinthians 14:1-3).

5) History indicates that tongues did cease. Tongues are not mentioned at all by the Post-Apostolic Fathers. Other writers such as Justin Martyr, Origen, Chrysostom, and Augustine considered tongues something that happened only in the earliest days of the Church.

6) Current observation confirms that the miracle of tongues has ceased. If the gift were still available today, there would be no need for missionaries to attend language school. Missionaries would be able to travel to any country and speak any language fluently, just as the apostles were able to speak in Acts 2. As for the miracle gift of healing, we see in Scripture that healing was associated with the ministry of Jesus and the apostles (Luke 9:1-2). And we see that as the era of the apostles drew to a close, healing, like tongues, became less frequent. The Apostle Paul, who raised Eutychus from the dead (Acts 20:9-12), did not heal Epaphroditus (Philippians 2:25-27), Trophimus (2 Timothy 4:20), Timothy (1 Timothy 5:23), or even himself (2 Corinthians 12:7-9). The reasons for Paul's "failures to heal" are 1) the gift was never intended to make every Christian well, but to authenticate apostleship; and 2) the authority of the apostles had been sufficiently proved, making further miracles unnecessary.

EQUALITY OF THE THREE PERSONS

We've studied Father, Son and Holy Spirit. One more of our claims needs to be addressed; that of the equality of the three:

"God is infinite and perfect, eternally existing in three equal persons."

In what sense are they equal? They are all equally endowed with all of the attributes of Personhood and Deity. Matthew 28:19: Therefore go and teach all nations, baptizing them in the name of the Father and of the Son and of the Holy Spirit.

To Repeat some of our earlier material

Unity of the One Being of Father, Son and Holy Spirit

Accordingly, therefore, there is that in the Father which constitutes him the Father and not the Son; there is that in the Son which constitutes Him the Son and not the Father; and there is that in the Holy Spirit which constitutes Him the Holy Spirit and not either the Father or the Son. Wherefore the Father is the Begetter, the Son is the Begotten, and the Holy Spirit is the one proceeding from the Father and the Son. Therefore, because these three persons in the Godhead are in a state of unity, there is but one Lord God Almighty and His name one.

John 1:18, John 15:26, John 17:11, John 17:21, Zechariah 14:9

Identity and Cooperation in the Godhead

The Father, the Son and the Holy Spirit are never identical as to Person; nor confused as to relation; nor divided in respect to the Godhead; nor opposed as to cooperation. The Son is in the Father and the Father is in the Son as to relationship. The Son is with the Father and the Father is with the Son, as to fellowship. The Father is not from the Son, but the Son is from the Father, as to authority. The Holy Spirit is from the Father and the Son proceeding, as to nature, relationship, cooperation and authority. Hence, neither Person in the Godhead either exists or works separately or independently of the others. (John 5:17-30, John 5:32, John 5:37, John 8:17,18)

The Other Charismatic Problem, Positive Confession (from Got Questions Ministries)

"Positive confession is the practice of saying aloud what you want to happen with the expectation that God will make it a reality. It's popular among prosperity gospel adherents who claim that words have spiritual power and that, if we speak aloud the right words with the right faith, we can gain riches and health, bind Satan, and accomplish anything we want. To confess positively is to speak words that we believe or want to believe, thus making them reality. This is opposed to negative confession, which is to acknowledge hardships, poverty, and illness and thus (supposedly) accept them and refuse the ease, wealth, and health God has planned for us.

There are several things wrong with this philosophy. The most dangerous is the belief that words have a kind of spiritual, magical power that we can use to get what we want. The practice borrows not from biblical truths, but from a new age concept called the "law of attraction." It teaches that "like attracts like"—a positive statement or thought will draw a positive reaction. Everything is imbued with God's presence and power—not "God" as the omnipresent Creator, but "god" in a Hindu/pantheistic way. The net result is the idea that our words hold the power to force God to give us what we want— a heretical belief. Additionally, the results attributed to positive confession are powered by the faith of the individual. This leads to the old belief that illness and poverty are a type of punishment for sin (in this case, lack of faith). John 9:1-3 and the entire book of Job refute this soundly.

The second problem is that the prosperity gospel misinterprets the promises of God. "Confession" is agreeing with what God has said; "positive confession" is demanding human desires. People who push positive confession say that the practice is merely restating God's promises as given in the Bible. But they don't differentiate between universal promises God made to all His followers (e.g., Philippians 4:19) and personal promises made to individuals at a certain time for a particular purpose (e.g., Jeremiah 29:11). They also misinterpret the promises God does give us, refusing to accept that God's plan for our lives may not match up with our own (Isaiah 55:9). A carefree, perfect life is the antithesis of what Jesus said the Christian life would look like—and the lives that His followers lived. Jesus didn't promise prosperity; He promised hardship (Matthew 8:20). He didn't promise that our every want would be fulfilled; He promised we'd have what we need (Philippians 4:19). He didn't promise peace in a family; He promised that families would have problems as some chose to follow Him and some didn't (Matthew 10:34-36). And He didn't promise health; He promised to fulfill His plan for us and grace in the trials (2 Corinthians 12:7-10).

Another issue with positive confession is that, although the "confessions" are understood to refer to things in the future, many of the statements are simply lies. Certainly, verbally affirming one's faith in God and deliverance by the sacrifice of Jesus is good. But proclaiming, "I always obey God," or, "I am wealthy," is deceptive and possibly against the very will of the God we are to cling to. Especially disturbing are the "confessions" about other people. God has given each of us the freedom to serve Him or rebel against Him in our individual ways; claiming otherwise is foolish.

Finally, the Bible is very clear that "negative confession" does not negate God's blessings. The Psalms are filled with cries to God for deliverance, and Psalm 55:22 and 1 Peter 5:7 exhort us follow that example. Even Jesus went before the Heavenly Father with a clear eye on the situation and a request for aid (Matthew 26:39). The God of the Bible is not a cosmic Santa Claus (James 4:1-3). He is a loving Father who wants to be involved in His children's lives—the good and the bad. It is when we humble ourselves and ask for help that He gives us either release from the circumstances or strength to get through them.

Does positive confession have any value? In a way. Those who are confident they can solve a problem are generally more relaxed and creative. An optimistic mood has been shown to improve health. And happy people often have enough emotional distance between themselves and others to pick up on subtle clues which could lead to successful personal and business transactions. In addition, consistently voicing one's goals keeps those goals on the forefront; those who constantly think about getting more money will act accordingly.

The dangers of positive confession far outweigh the benefits. All of the advantages we've listed are psychological and somewhat physiological—not spiritual. The only spiritual benefit to be had is the fact that people who expect God to move are more likely to see God's hand in situations. But words are not magic. Our role with our Heavenly Father is not to demand, but to ask for help and to trust. And to realize that our blessings are not dependent on the strength of our faith, but on His plan and His power."
From my own personal experience, Positive Confession, also known as "name it and claim it," can be destructive to one's faith. Contrary to what some pastors will tell you, sometimes God does say no and if all you have is the kind of faith found in the Word of Faith Movement (Prosperity Gospel), you will easily find yourself wondering if your faith is defective. As you study

your Bible you will find the Book of Job. That book is the 800-pound gorilla in the room when it comes to positive confession. Sometimes you will have to suffer. As Spurgeon said, "There are no crown wearers in Heaven who were not cross bearers on earth."

I mentioned my personal experience...Here is my story on that: As a child, I suffered from focal epileptic seizures; for years we prayed for healing and confessed that I was healed, yet every month I was off to the neurologist for another EEG Test and more anti-seizure medication. Eventually, I realized that my naming and claiming my healing was not getting me anywhere and it could not; only God, Himself, has creative power in His words and only He can bring wholeness to the body with a spoken word. I finally resigned myself to being epileptic and never again confessed a healing I did not have, though I did still pray for it. Years later, according to His gracious purposes, the Lord God did decide to grant that healing and I have been seizure free for 17 years. Right there, in that last sentence, is the key, Beloved. You must understand that everything that God does is according to the Counsel of His Own Will and according to His purposes in grace.

Lesson 6 Man, Sin, and Salvation

Man is the special creation of God, made in His own image. He created them male and female as the crowning work of His creation. (The gift of gender is thus part of the goodness of God's creation.) In the beginning man was innocent of sin and was endowed by his Creator with freedom of choice. By his free choice man sinned against God and brought sin into the human race. Through the temptation of Satan man transgressed the command of God, and fell from his original innocence whereby his posterity inherit a nature and an environment inclined toward sin. Therefore, as soon as we are capable of moral action, we become transgressors and are under condemnation. Only the grace of God can bring man into His holy fellowship and enable man to fulfill the creative purpose of God.

Genesis 1:26-30; 2:5,7,18-22; 3; 9:6; Psalms 1; 8:3-6; 32:1-5; 51:5; Isaiah 6:5; Jeremiah 17:5; Matthew 16:26; Acts 17:26- 31; Romans 1:19-32; 3:10-18,23; 5:6,12,19; 6:6; 7:14-25; 8:14-18,29; 1 Corinthians 1:21-31; 15:19,21-22; Ephesians 2:1-22; Colossians 1:21-22; 3:9-11.

Sin, Original and Personal

Sin came into the world through the disobedience of our first parents, and death by sin. We believe that sin is of two kinds: original sin or depravity, and actual or personal sin.

Original sin, or depravity, is that corruption of the nature of all the offspring of Adam by reason of which everyone is very far gone from original righteousness or the pure state of our first parents at the time of their creation, is averse to God, is without spiritual life, and inclined to evil, and that continually. Our fallen nature continues with us until our glorification by Christ in the New Heaven and the New Earth.

Actual, or personal, sin is a voluntary violation of a known law of God by a morally responsible person (There no particular age set forth in Scripture for this moral responsibility. That being said, every individual is, at some point in their life accountable to God for their sins and are faced with the choice to respond or not.) It is therefore not to be confused with involuntary and inescapable shortcomings, infirmities, faults, mistakes, failures, or other deviations from the standard of perfect conduct that are the residual effects of the Fall.

Original sin: Genesis 3; 6:5; Job 15:14; Psalm 51:5; Jeremiah 17:9-10; Mark 7:21-23; Romans 1:18-25; 5:12-14; 7:1-8:9; 1 Corinthians 3:1-4; Galatians 5:16-25; 1 John 1:7-8

Personal sin: Matthew 22:36-40 {with 1 John 3:4}; John 8:34- 36; 16:8-9; Romans 3:23; 6:15-23; 8:18-24; 14:23; 1 John 1:9- 2:4; 3:7-10)

This Doctrine of Original Sin leads us to discuss Total Depravity...

Let's start with the obvious question, what is Total Depravity? Total depravity is a phrase that is used to summarize what the Bible teaches about the natural spiritual condition of fallen man (By that I mean the spiritual condition we are born in because of Original Sin). It's the "T" in the acronym TULIP, which is commonly used to enumerate the five points of Calvinism and the "T" that is used in FACTS to enumerate the 5 points of Classical Evangelical Arminianism.

This isn't a comfortable topic; it certainly isn't something that we discuss at parties in "polite society" and it, most definitely, isn't some niggling little detail that can be overlooked. It entails what may well be the most taboo word in our morally relativistic society, sin. You are a sinner and so am I (yes I really did just go there) and we are all in big trouble because of it.

Total Depravity, though often misunderstood, acknowledges that the Bible teaches that every part of man—the mind, will, emotions, and flesh are corrupted by sin. This is a result of the sin in Genesis 3:6. This is to say that sin affects all of our being—who we are and what we do. Sin has so penetrated us, going to the core of our being, so that everything is polluted by sin. Any good deeds that we do, any righteousness that we bring to God is like filthy rags. (Isaiah 64:6) To give you an idea of how disgusting sin is to God, how utterly repugnant it is, I will share with you what the Hebrew literally says;

filthy rags is the cleaned up version for church. Literally, in the Hebrew, it says our righteousness is as a menstrual cloth. I realize that what I just said is shocking and it should be. We don't take sin seriously enough; you don't and I don't and that's just reality. None of us lives in constant awareness of just how awful our sin really is. If we did, we would most probably never leave the church. Let's move on...

In the bullet points below, we have summarized the Doctrine of Total Depravity

o The heart is deceitful and desperately wicked (Jeremiah 17:9)

o We are born dead in our transgressions and sins (Psalm 51:5, Psalm 58:3 and Ephesians 2:1-5)

o We are held captive to a love for sin (John 3:19 and John 8:34)

o There is no one who seeks for God (Romans 3:10-11)

o Man loves the darkness (John 3:19)

o Men do not understand the things of God (1 Corinthians 2:14)

o As a result, men suppress the Truth of God in unrighteousness (Romans 1:18) and continue to live in sin.

o Because of the totally depraved nature of man, he continues to live in sin and this sinful life actually seems right to him (Proverbs 14:12)

o Depravity is so pervasive that, by nature, we reject the Message of the Gospel as foolish (1 Corinthians 1:18) and our minds, naturally do not submit to God because it is unable to do so. (Romans 8:7)

Paul summarizes Total Depravity this way (Romans 3:9-18)

o No one is without sin

o No one seeks after God

o There is no one is good

o Our speech is corrupted by sin

o Man's actions are corrupted by sin

o And above all, man has no fear of God

The summary verse of the Doctrine of Total Depravity is Romans 3:12 which tells us that there is no one who does good, not a single one. Total Depravity does not mean that man is as sinful or wicked as is possible to be (Utter Depravity) and it also does not mean that we are totally without a sense of right and wrong. It doesn't even mean we cannot do things that would be considered good by human standards. It does, however, mean that we are incapable, on our own, of pleasing God.

We are not without hope: prior to the cross, God made a way for us to deal with the pollutions of sin through Faith and Obedience combined with the Levitical Sacrifices. After the cross, we are justified by faith and empowered

unto holiness by the indwelling Holy Spirit, Himself being God, who is the seal of our redemption and the guarantee of our eternal home in Heaven.
Salvation
Salvation involves the redemption of the whole man, and is offered freely to all who accept Jesus Christ as Lord and Savior, who by His own blood obtained eternal redemption for the believer. In its broadest sense salvation includes regeneration, justification, sanctification, and glorification. There is no salvation apart from personal faith in Jesus Christ as Lord. Let us look, for a moment, to the Baptist Faith and Message:
A. Regeneration, or the new birth, is a work of God's grace whereby believers become new creatures in Christ Jesus. It is a change of heart wrought by the Holy Spirit through conviction of sin, to which the sinner responds in repentance toward God and faith in the Lord Jesus Christ. Repentance and faith are inseparable experiences of grace.
Repentance is a genuine turning from sin toward God. Faith is the acceptance of Jesus Christ and commitment of the entire personality to Him as Lord and Savior.
B. Justification is God's gracious and full acquittal upon principles of His righteousness of all sinners who repent and believe in Christ. Justification brings the believer unto a relationship of peace and favor with God.
C. Sanctification is the experience, beginning in regeneration, by which the believer is set apart to God's purposes, and is enabled to progress toward moral and spiritual maturity through the presence and power of the Holy Spirit dwelling in him. Growth in grace should continue throughout the regenerate person's life.
D. Glorification is the culmination of salvation and is the final blessed and abiding state of the redeemed.
Genesis 3:15; Exodus 3:14-17; 6:2-8; Matthew 1:21; 4:17; 16:21-26; 27:22-28:6; Luke 1:68-69; 2:28-32; John 1:11-14,29; 3:3-21,36; 5:24; 10:9,28-29; 15:1-16; 17:17; Acts 2:21; 4:12; 15:11; 16:30-31; 17:30-31; 20:32; Romans 1:16- 18; 2:4; 3:23-25; 4:3ff.; 5:8-10; 6:1-23; 8:1- 18,29-39; 10:9- 10,13; 13:11-14; 1 Corinthians 1:18,30; 6:19-20; 15:10; 2 Corinthians 5:17-20; Galatians 2:20; 3:13; 5:22- 25; 6:15; Ephesians 1:7; 2:8-22; 4:11-16; Philippians 2:12- 13; Colossians 1:9- 22; 3:1ff.; 1 Thessalonians 5:23-24; 2 Timothy 1:12; Titus 2:11-14; Hebrews 2:1-3; 5:8-9; 9:24- 28; 11:1-12:8,14; James 2:14-26; 1 Peter 1:2-23; 1 John 1:6- 2:11; Revelation 3:20; 21:1-22:5.

God's Purpose of Grace
Election is the gracious purpose of God, according to which He regenerates, justifies, sanctifies, and glorifies sinners. It is consistent with the free agency of man, and comprehends all the means in connection with the end. It is the

glorious display of God's sovereign goodness, and is infinitely wise, holy, and unchangeable. It excludes boasting and promotes humility.

Genesis 12:1-3; Exodus 19:5-8; 1 Samuel 8:4-7,19-22; Isaiah 5:1-7; Jeremiah 31:31ff.; Matthew 16:18-19; 21:28- 45; 24:22,31; 25:34; Luke 1:68-79; 2:29-32; 19:41-44; 24:44- 48; John 1:12- 14; 3:16; 5:24; 6:44-45,65; 10:27- 29; 15:16; 17:6,12,17-18; Acts 20:32; Romans 5:9-10; 8:28- 39; 10:12-15; 11:5-7,26-36; 1 Corinthians 1:1-2; 15:24- 28; Ephesians 1:4-23; 2:1-10; 3:1-11; Colossians 1:12-14; 2 Thessalonians 2:13-14; 2 Timothy 1:12; 2:10,19; Hebrews 11:39–12:2; James 1:12; 1 Peter 1:2-5,13; 2:4-10; 1 John 1:7- 9; 2:19; 3:2.

Chosen For Salvation/Unconditional Sovereign Election

On both sides of the soteriological coin (Calvinist and Arminian), we see that God chooses some to be saved from wrath and damnation, so that is not debated. What is debated however, are the twin doctrines of election and grace. I would like to look, briefly at these...

The Belgic Confession teaches us:

Of Eternal Election

We believe that all the posterity of Adam being thus fallen into perdition and ruin, by the sin of our first parents, God then did manifest himself such as he is; that is to say, merciful and just: Merciful, since he delivers and preserves from this perdition all, whom he, in his eternal and unchangeable counsel of mere goodness, has elected in Christ Jesus our Lord, without any respect to their works: Just, in leaving others in the fall and perdition wherein they have involved themselves.

The Scriptures Declare:

1.   II Thessalonians 2:13: God chose you from the beginning unto salvation in sanctification of the Spirit and belief of the truth.

1.   Matthew 24:24: There shall arise false Christs, and false prophets, and shall show great signs and wonders; so as to lead astray, if possible, even the elect.

1.   Matthew 24:31: And they (the angels) shall gather together His elect from the four winds, from one end of heaven to the other.

1.   Mark 13:20: For the elect's sake, whom He chose, He shortened those days (at the destruction of Jerusalem).

1.   I Thessalonians 1:4: Knowing, brethren, beloved of God, your election.

1.   Romans 11:7: The election obtained it, and the rest were hardened.

1.   I Timothy 5:21: I charge thee in the sight of God, and Jesus Christ, and the elect angels.

1.   Romans 8:33: Who shall lay anything to the charge of God's elect?

1.   Romans 11:5: (In comparison with Elijah's time) Even so at the present time also there is a remnant according to the election of grace.

1.	II Timothy 2:10: I endure all things for the elect's sake.

1.	Titus 1:1: Paul, a servant of God, and an apostle of Jesus Christ, according to the faith of God's elect.

1.	I Peter 1:1: Peter, an apostle of Jesus Christ, to the elect.

1.	I Peter 5:13: She that is in Babylon, elect together with you.

1.	I Peter 2:9: But ye are an elect race.

1.	I Thessalonians 5:9: For God appointed us not unto wrath, but unto the obtaining of salvation through our Lord Jesus Christ.

1.	Acts 13:48: And as the Gentiles heard this, they were glad, and glorified the word of God; and as many as were ordained to eternal life believed.

1.	John 17:9: I (Jesus) pray not for the world, but for those whom thou hast given me; for they are thine.

1.	John 6:37: All that the Father giveth me shall come unto me.

1.	John 6:65: No man can come unto me except it be given unto him of the Father.

1.	John 13:18: I speak not of you all; I know whom I have chosen.

1.	John 15:16: Ye did not choose me, but I chose you.

1.	Psalm 105:6: Ye children of Jacob, His chosen ones.

1.	Romans. 9:23: Vessels of mercy, which He afore prepared unto glory.

Ephesians 1:3-15
3 Blessed be the God and Father of our Lord Jesus Christ,
who hath blessed us with all spiritual blessings in heavenly places in Christ: 4 According as he hath chosen us in him before the foundation of the world, that we should be holy and without blame before him in love: 5 Having predestinated us unto the adoption of children by Jesus Christ to himself, according to the good pleasure of his will, 6 To the praise of the glory of his grace, wherein he hath made us accepted in the beloved. 7 In whom we have redemption through his blood, the forgiveness of sins, according to the riches of his grace; 8 Wherein he hath abounded toward us in all wisdom and prudence; 9 Having made known unto us the mystery of his will, according to his good pleasure which he hath purposed in himself:
10 That in the dispensation of the fullness of times he might gather together in one all things in Christ, both which are in heaven, and which are on earth; even in him: 11 In whom also we have obtained an inheritance, being predestinated according to the purpose of him who worketh all things after the counsel of his own will: 12 That we should be to the praise of his glory, who first trusted in Christ. 13 In whom ye also trusted, after that ye heard the word of truth, the gospel of your salvation: in whom also after that ye believed, ye were sealed with that Holy Spirit of promise, 14 Which is the earnest of our inheritance until the redemption of the purchased possession, unto the praise of his glory.

• Romans 9:11-14

11 (For the children being not yet born, neither having done any good or evil, that the purpose of God according to election might stand, not of works, but of him that calleth;) 12 It was said unto her, The elder shall serve the younger. 13 As it is written, Jacob have I loved, but Esau have I hated. 14 What shall we say then? Is there unrighteousness with God? God forbid.

I almost feel like commenting further would be to presume upon the Scripture as if I, who am less than the least of the righteous could add anything to the Word of the Lord. On many occasions, I have heard Dr. Sproul say that the question should not be "Is Jesus the only way? or Why is Jesus the only way? but that the question, rather, ought to be, "Why should there be any way of salvation at all?" I would say the same of election. It is no marvel that God should save some and allow others to be damned; it is a marvel that He should save any at all. *Further, for those of who believe that we are elect, that election should cause fear and trembling; it is never anything to boast about as though we are somehow superior to others.*

We believe and teach that man is totally depraved and unable to choose to do right; in our flesh dwells no good thing (Romans 7:18), there is none who does what is right on his own (Romans 3:10). In Isaiah 64:6 we see that our righteousness is as filthy rags. Now let me be blunt; that is the very cleaned up version that you will see in your Bible. What it actually says is that all our righteousness is like menstrual cloths, not a pretty thing to think about. We are, basically, hopeless and helpless. But...

"God, before the foundation of the world, chose to make certain individuals the objects of His unmerited favor or special grace (Mark 13:20; Ephesians 1:4-5; Revelation 13:8; Revelation 17:8). These individuals from every tribe, tongue and nation were chosen by God for adoption, not because of anything they would do but because of His sovereign will (Romans 9:11-13; Romans 9:16; Romans 10:20; 1 Corinthians 1:27-29; 2 Timothy 1:9). God could have chosen to save all men (He certainly has the power and authority to do so), and He could have chosen to save no one (He is under no obligation to save anyone). He instead chose to save some and leave others to the consequences of their sin (Exodus 33:19; Deuteronomy 7:6-7; Romans 9:10- 24; Acts 13:48; 1 Peter 2:8)." {gotquestions.org}

I would be a first rate liar if I said this wasn't difficult, especially since I am fairly certain that some people, who were very close to me in life, were most probably not elect. Being absolutely 100% honest with you, Beloved, I have not a clue why God saves some and not others; neither do I have even the tiniest fraction of a clue how He decided whom He would elect and, in my estimation, anyone who says they do is a liar. There are certain things which God keeps only to Himself and, while we may someday get a clue and understand why He allows things to be thus and so, we sometimes must do what is, honestly, difficult sometimes and that is to trust that the Holy God knows exactly what He is doing and will get the glory due Him alone.

Sovereign Election and Definite Atonement

The certainty of Sovereign Election necessarily requires a certain, definite atonement. (It is important to note that, as part of our affirmation of Reformed Soteriology, we affirm and teach the Doctrine of Definite Atonement.) This doctrine, Definite Atonement, is sometimes called Limited Atonement but I think that nomenclature is unnecessarily offensive to some and can be deceptive. Many people who hear the term, Limited Atonement, automatically assume that it means the atoning work of Christ was limited in power, which, if true, would de facto render such atonement useless. Instead the terms Definite Atonement and
Particular Redemption are the more accurate verbiage to use. Definite Atonement implies the certainty of redemption, and we can be sure that since the Father decreed that there would be a redemption, it will most definitely come to pass; Particular Redemption, being the other half of that coin, implies that a particular people will be redeemed and we can see the accuracy of this implication in "Elect Israel" in the Old Testament. God chose them based on the good pleasure of His will which is the same methodology He uses in our election.

Before we discuss why sovereign election demands a definite and particular redemption, we need to understand some terms, which differ from definite atonement:

Universal Salvation claims that Christ obtained salvation for everyone in the world and that the Holy Spirit applies salvation to everyone in the world so that all are saved. By default, we must reject this doctrine as heretical since, if all will be saved, the Gospel is unneeded, hell is rendered non-existent, and the Holiness of God would be rendered utterly pointless. In point of fact, if Universal Salvation is true then the life of holiness and being conformed to the image of Christ required by the Bible becomes a cruel demand.

General Ransom holds that, although Christ obtained salvation for everyone in the world, the Holy Spirit applies salvation only to those who come to faith so that only these are actually saved. On the surface, this sounds really good (and even accurate) but sovereign electing grace poses a significant problem here; if everyone can come to faith and be saved, what is the point of election? We will come back answer that question in a bit.

Definite Atonement holds that Christ obtained salvation only for the elect and that the Holy Spirit applies salvation only to the elect. Another way to say this is, The Atoning Work of the cross is, in fact, sufficient that all might be saved, but it is only effectual for the elect that their redemption might be guaranteed.

For whom, then, did Jesus die?

This is, to borrow from the culture, the $64,000 question. Christ died a substitutionary death on the cross, this much is certain. For whom was He a substitute?

The Scripture tells us that God has chosen a people for Himself, out of all of fallen humanity, and that these are His Elect, whom He has graciously chosen to redeem. How many will be redeemed is a number known only to the Godhead. It is for this purpose of redemption that Christ is come into the world. (John 6:37-40; 10:27-29; 11:51-52; Romans 8:28-39; Ephesians 1:3-14; 1Peter 1:20).

In Scripture, Christ is regularly said to have died for particular groups or persons. It is clear that the implication is that His death fully secured their salvation. (John 10:15-18,27- 29; Romans 5:8-10; 8:32; Galatians 2:20; 3:13-14; 4:4-5; 1 John 4:9-10; Revelation 1:4-6; 5:9-10). Facing His suffering on the cross, Jesus prayed only for those whom the Father had given him, not for the "world" (i.e., the rest of humanity; John 17:9,20). It is for these that the Penal Substitutionary Atonement is efficacious.

Notwithstanding, it is also important that we affirm the free offer of Jesus Christ in the gospel alongside the doctrine of definite atonement. (I can say with many of the Reformers, both sovereign election and free will are taught in scripture and it is only my own folly that prevents me from reconciling the two.) It is a certainty that whoever comes to Christ in faith will find mercy (John 6:35,47-51,54-57; Romans 1:16; 10:8-13). Those whom God has chosen hear Christ's offer, and through hearing it, they are effectually called by the Holy Spirit. Both the invitation and the effectual calling flow from Christ's sin-bearing death, that is, His substitutionary atonement for His elect. Those who reject the offer of Christ do so because they choose to (Matthew 22:1-7; John 3:18), so their final doom is their own fault; in a sense, they have refused to bow the knee to Christ and say to Him, "Lord, let Thy will be done." and so, He says to them "Let thine own will be done" and grants them their eternal abode in the place of the damned. We, who "receive" Christ do so with thanksgiving and all praise due Him, knowing that all we contribute to our redemption is the sin that made it necessary and that our own election is for His Glory alone.

But this begs the nagging question: Are People Predestined to Heaven and Hell?

First let's define the term: predestination is how we translate the Greek word proorizo, which appears six times in the New Testament (Acts 4:28; Romans 8:29-30; 1 Corinthians 2:7; Ephesians 1:5,11). In some instances, it refers to God's foreordination of all the events of world history (Acts 4:28; 1 Corinthians 2:7). In others, it refers to God's decision, made before the world existed, regarding the final destiny of individual sinners. Specifically, it is seen of those chosen for salvation and eternal life (Romans 8:29-30; Ephesians 1:5,11), as opposed to those who will ultimately be condemned to eternal judgment. Many have pointed out, however, that Scripture also ascribes to God an advance decision about those who in the final analysis are not saved (Romans 9:6-29; 1 Peter 2:8; Jude 4). By predestining only some to salvation, it would seem that God necessarily consigns the remainder to destruction. In light of this, it has become common in many circles to teach a doctrine known as Double Predestination, which sees God's predestination as including both his decision to save some from sin (election) and his decision to condemn the rest for their sin (reprobation). In the interest of total honesty, I would be an absolute liar if I claimed to understand God's Electing Grace including redemption and reprobation.

Election and Predestination is, candidly, a difficult doctrine to wrap one's mind around. A number of denominations speak of predestination (or election) on the basis of God's foreknowledge of faith being found in certain individuals. They teach that God knew beforehand that certain people would freely choose Christ as their Savior once they had heard the gospel, and conclude that on this basis God then elects them to salvation. In this sense, foreknowledge is passive foresight on God's part of what individuals will chose of their own free will without God compelling them. God then predetermines people's destinies, responding to what He has seen will take place.

This brings up the niggling problem of the word prognosko. The Greek word prognōskō, translated "foreknew" in Romans 8:29 and 11:2 can also mean "fore-loved" and "fore-acknowledged" (see 1 Peter 1:20, where prognōskō is rendered "chosen before"). Passages such as the above would seem to make it clear that prognōskō expresses foreknowledge of a person, not foreknowledge of mere facts about the future or a person's life choices. Assuming the accuracy of that, then the New Testament teaches that God has elected on the basis of his fore-love and affection for those to whom he gives eternal life.

Because Adam is our Federal Head and we are all born dead in sin, no one who hears the gospel will ever come to repentance and faith without the inner quickening that only God can impart, which we naturally refer to as Regeneration. (Ephesians 2:4-10). Jesus said, "no one can come to me unless the Father has enabled him" (John 6:65; John 6:44; 10:25-28). If God looks into the future to see what choices we will make on our own, then we are all damned because none will, on his own, come to Christ. Absent the intervention of the Holy Spirit imputing the life and righteousness of Christ to us, we would forever be doomed to our sin.

So then, humanity is totally depraved and, having no desire to seek God, will not come to Him. God chooses, based on the counsel of His own will, a people to save from His wrath and their just damnation and it is for this people, in particular, that Christ died.

Of necessity, Definite Atonement requires Irresistible Grace.
The Doctrine of Irresistible Grace (http://theopedia.com) "Those who obtain the new birth do so, not because they wanted to obtain it, but because of the sovereign discriminating grace of God. That is, men are overcome by grace, not finally because their consciences were more tender or their faith more tenacious than that of other men. Rather, the willingness and ability to do God's will are evidence of God's own faithfulness to save men from the power and the penalty of sin, and since man is so corrupt that he will not decide and cannot be wooed to follow after God, sovereign efficacious grace is required to convert him. This is done by the regeneration of the Holy Spirit whereby a fallen man who has heard the gospel is made willing and necessarily turns to Christ in God-given faith."

Major Scriptures related to the Doctrine of Irresistible Grace:
1.   John 6:37, 39 (ESV): "All that the Father gives me willcome to me.... And this is the will of him who sent me, that I should lose nothing of all that he has given me, but raise it up on the last day."
1.   John 6:44-45 (ESV): "No one can come to me unless the Father who sent me draws him.... Everyone who has heard and learned from the Father comes to me."
1.   John 6:65 (ESV): "No one can come to me unless it is granted him by the Father."
1.   Romans 8:28, 30 (ESV) "Those whom [God] predestined he also called, and those whom he called he also justified, and those whom he justified he also glorified".
All that the Father gives will come...what does this mean? It means, as John MacArthur points out, that in eternity past the Father determined to give, to the Son, a redeemed humanity as a love gift and every person that the LORD God has sovereignly elected unto salvation will come to the feet of the Son, the Lord of Glory, Jesus Christ. On a certain level, this is a mystery for we are not clearly told, in Scripture, how this comes to pass, yet the Scripture does in fact teach that it will happen.

One thing that we want to point out is a particular Greek word in John 6:44 and that word is ἕλκω, helkô and the word, generally has the connotation of dragging (John. 18:10; 21:6; 21:11; Acts 16:19; 21:30; James. 2:6). As a consequence, we can assume that it means that this drawing cannot be resisted. *This is not to say that God's grace can never be resisted under any circumstances. Rather, as Dr. Sproul teaches us, "The idea is that God's grace is so powerful that it has the capacity to overcome our natural resistance to it.* It is not that the Holy Spirit drags people kicking and screaming to Christ against their wills. The Holy Spirit changes the inclination and disposition of our wills, so that whereas we were previously unwilling to embrace Christ, now we are willing, and more than willing."

We learned, in the section on Total Depravity/Total Inability, that man is, of his own accord, not only unwilling but also unable to come to Christ; it's kind of a vicious circle: man cannot come to Christ because he does not want to and he does not want to because he cannot. Thankfully, on the other side of that coin is the fact that God, the Father, changes the desires of our hearts; He creates a new heart where the old obstinately disinterested one used to be and we are now capable of seeing the beauty of the Glorious Prince of Heaven and and are so desirous of the Redeemer that we willingly come and bow at the Throne of Grace.

Some would object to this doctrine, yet I will answer their objection with the words of Paul, "Nay but, O man, who art thou that repliest against God? Shall the thing formed say to him that formed it, "Why hast thou made me thus?" (Romans 9:20) or, perhaps, the words of Isaiah, "Who hath directed the Spirit of

the LORD, or being his counseller hath taught him?"

I suspect that many of the objections to this doctrine come from those who do not really understand it. Let us turn then, to our friends from Got Questions Ministries for some wise instruction:

"The reason this doctrine is called "irresistible" grace is that it always results in the intended outcome, the salvation of the person it is given to. It is important to realize that the act of being regenerated or "born again" cannot be separated from the act of believing the gospel. Ephesians 2:1-10 makes this clear. There is a connection between the act of being made alive by God (Ephesians 2:1, 5) and the result of being saved by grace. (Ephesians 2:5, 8). This is because everything pertaining to salvation, including the faith to believe, is an act of God's grace. The reason God's grace is irresistible and efficacious (always bringing forth the desired result) is that God "has delivered us from the power of darkness and conveyed us into" His kingdom (Colossians 1:13). Or, as Psalm 3:8 puts it, "Salvation belongs to the Lord."

To understand the doctrine of "irresistible grace," it is important to recognize that this is a special grace given only to those God has chosen for salvation (His elect) and is different from what is known as "common grace" which God bestows on both believer and unbeliever. While there are many aspects of common grace, including life and all that is necessary to sustain it, common grace is what is often referred to as the "outward call of God." This is God's revelation of Himself given to all men through the light of creation and their consciences. It also includes the general call of the gospel that goes out anytime the gospel message is preached. This call can be resisted and rejected by those that receive it. (Matthew 22:14; Romans 1:18-32).

However, God also gives an "inward call" which always results in salvation. This is the call of God that Jesus spoke of in John 6:37-47. The certainty of this inward call is seen in John 6:37: "All that the Father gives Me will come to Me, and the one who comes to Me I will by no means cast out." John 6:44

confirms this: "No one can come to me unless the Father who sent me draws him and I will raise him up at the last day."

To summarize, Irresistible, or efficacious, Grace is the consequence of the transforming power of the Holy Spirit. To borrow from the popular culture, it is, in a sense, when God makes you an offer you can't refuse; it is that gift of grace which allows us to become the Bride, without spot or wrinkle, who is suitable for the Bridegroom, the Crown Prince of Heaven.

The Security of the Believer

All true believers endure to the end. Those whom God has accepted in Christ, and sanctified by His Spirit, will never fall away from the state of grace, but shall persevere to the end. Believers may fall into sin through neglect and temptation, whereby they grieve the Spirit, impair their graces and comforts, and bring reproach on the cause of Christ and temporal judgments on themselves; yet they shall be kept by the power of God through faith unto salvation.

Ephesians 4:30 tells us that believers are "sealed for the day of redemption." If believers did not have eternal security, the sealing could not truly be unto the day of redemption, but only to the day of sinning, apostasy, or disbelief. John 3:15-16 tells us that whoever believes in Jesus Christ will "have eternal life." If a person were to be promised eternal life, but then have it taken away, it was never "eternal" to begin with. If eternal security is not true, the promises of eternal life in the Bible would be in error.

The most powerful argument for eternal security is Romans 8:38-39, "For I am convinced that neither death nor life, neither angels nor demons, neither the present nor the future, nor any powers, neither height nor depth, nor anything else in all creation, will be able to separate us from the love of God that is in Christ Jesus our Lord." Our eternal security is based on God's love for those whom He has redeemed. Our eternal security is purchased by Christ, promised by the Father, and sealed by the Holy Spirit.

This Doctrine is formally called the Perseverance of the Saints but it is frequently referred to as Eternal Security or (pejoratively) Once Saved Always Saved.

Eternal security is the teaching that a Christian cannot lose his salvation because he is "eternally secure" in the work of Christ. Unfortunately, this teaching is sometimes a source of problems within Christian circles. Some Christians believe that if you hold to eternal security, you are purposely promoting a license to sin. On the other hand, some Christians believe that if you don't believe in eternal security, you have to keep your salvation by works. Both sides often misrepresent the other, and instead of being gracious on this debatable issue (as we are commanded to be in Romans 14:1-12), people accuse each other of being unbiblical.

First and foremost, Eternal Security is not a license to sin.

Please understand that eternal security is not a license to sin. The Christian is regenerated. He is changed from within and is made a new creature (2 Cor. 5:17). Those who were indwelt by the Holy Spirit will war with their sin and not seek to abide in it. Those who declare that they are eternally secure and then go out and sin on purpose in any manner they so choose are probably not saved to begin with since this is contradictory to what Scripture teaches. 1 John 2:4 says, "The one who says, 'I have come to know Him,' and does not keep His commandments, is a liar, and the truth is not in him."

This does not, in any way, imply that we will never again sin; we can be certain that we will sin again because we are under the Federal Headship of Adam and will have a fallen nature until we are restored in the Kingdom. I want to give you 3 passages of Scripture regarding the Security of the Believer.

John 6:37-40

"All that the Father gives Me shall come to Me, and the one who comes to Me I will certainly not cast out. 38 "For I have come down from heaven, not to do My own will, but the will of Him who sent Me. 39 "And this is the will of Him who sent Me, that of all that He has given Me I lose nothing, but raise it up on the last day. 40 "For this is the will of My Father, that everyone who beholds the Son and believes in Him, may have eternal life; and I Myself will raise him up on the last day,"

John 10:27-28

"My sheep hear My voice, and I know them, and they follow Me; 28 and I give eternal life to them, and they shall never perish; and no one shall snatch them out of My hand,"

1 John 2:19

"They went out from us, but they were not really of us; for if they had been of us, they would have remained with us; but they went out, in order that it might be shown that they all are not of us."

I need to emphasize, with as much vigor as possible, that this does not mean that you can simply live however you like and still go to Heaven when you die. There will always be a struggle with sin and you will fail; so will I. As you mature in your discipleship, you will become more like Christ and so will hate your sin more and more. Some areas will be easier to resist sin and in other areas, it will feel like World War III. The comfort is that we are assured of a final victory.

3 Things the Doctrine of Eternal Security does not teach:

"1) Since we are 'saved', we can do what we want. It doesn't matter what kind of sin we commit. We are still going to go to heaven." This is a gross perversion of Eternal Security. ALL TRUE BELIEVERS will endure to the end. In Jude's epistle the Apostle advises that we contend vigorously for the faith and the word he uses is agonizomai. It is from this word that we derive agonize, and it is fitting because "Take up your cross and follow Me" is a death sentence and the flesh will not be overcome easily.

"2) We do not need to worry about helping our brothers and sisters remain faithful. "Hey, if they are saved, they will remain saved. We do not need to be our brother's keeper". If this were true, there would be no need for corporate worship or the preaching of the word.

"3) We can ignore all the Scriptures warning us to persevere to the very end. We don't need to persevere because if we are saved, we will remain saved." I cannot imagine that anyone seriously thinks that Eternal Security means this but I have heard it from some. Sanctification is both instantaneous and a process. We are admonished to work out our salvation with fear and trembling (Philippians 2:12) for a reason. The Holy Spirit does sanctify us but that does not leave us with no responsibility to work.

Lesson 7 Baptism and Communion
Believer's Baptism
Following the model displayed in the New Testament, Exploring the Truth takes the position that baptism is limited exclusively to the repentant believer who, having placed his faith and obedience, in Christ, and now wishes to publicly profess faith before the Household of the Faithful and to identify with the death, burial, and resurrection of our Lord through full, bodily immersion in water (except when medically not possible). We do not teach that baptism saves; rather we teach that this is the first step of obedience to the commands of our Lord and His Apostles. As a consequence of this, it is the position of Exploring the Truth that Paedobaptism is not valid as fulfillment of the Apostolic Mandate to "repent and be baptized (Acts 2:38)"

Defending Our Position
An excerpt from Baptist Distinctives...
"Ask most non-Baptists (and even some Baptists!) what is the Baptist distinctive and they likely will say, "Baptism of adults by immersion." Of course, there is no one Baptist distinctive. Why then do many people regard baptism as practiced by Baptists to be our distinctive? A possible reason is that Baptists are one of the very few denominations that practice believer's baptism by immersion and do so as a symbol of having been saved, not as a requirement for salvation. "

In previous centuries, rulers of both state and church launched persecutions against Baptists for this practice. In the face of such harsh resistance, as well as the inconvenience of immersion, why have Baptists stubbornly held to the belief in and practice of believer's immersion? The answer is found in basic Baptist convictions...

Baptism Is Only for Believers
The New Testament records that baptism always followed conversion, never preceded it, and it was not necessary for salvation (Acts 2:1-41; 8:36-39;

16:30-33). Since Baptists look to the Bible as our sole authority for faith and practice, we believe that baptism is only for those who have put their faith in Jesus Christ as Lord and Savior.

Furthermore, Baptists point out that in the New Testament a commitment to believe in and follow Jesus as Lord and Savior was always voluntary. Therefore, baptism as a sign of such commitment ought always to be voluntary.

Because of these convictions based on the Bible, Baptists do not baptize infants. This refusal has resulted in persecution. For example, Henry Dunster, the first president of Harvard University, was forced not only from his office but banished from Cambridge for refusing to have his infant children baptized in the state-supported church.

Baptism Is Only by Immersion

Although some early Baptists baptized by pouring or sprinkling water over a person, Baptists concluded that immersion of a person's entire body in water was the only biblical way to baptize. Therefore, in spite of persecution, inconvenience and ridicule, they began to practice baptism only by immersion. Today, that is the Baptist way throughout most of the world. It should also be noted that in some cases such as medical inability a pouring of water over the head would be considered a valid baptism.

The belief in immersion as the proper mode of baptism is based on the Bible for several reasons:

1.   The English word "baptize" comes from a word in the Greek language—the language in which the New Testament originally was written—that means "to dip, submerge, or immerse."

1.   John the Baptist baptized Jesus in the Jordan River by immersion as Jesus began his public ministry (Matthew 3:13-17; Mark 1:9-11).

1.   Christ's disciples in New Testament times baptized by immersion (Acts 8:36-39).

1.   Immersion is a means not only of declaring that Christ died, was buried and was resurrected to provide salvation but also of testifying about our own hope of resurrection (Romans 6:5).

1.   The New Testament teaches that immersion is a way to symbolize that a believer has died to an old way and is alive to walk a new way in Christ (Romans 6:3-4; Colossians 2:11-12).

Baptism Is Symbolic

Baptists believe that the Bible teaches that baptism is important but not necessary for salvation. For example, the thief on the cross (Luke 23:39-43), Saul on the Damascus road (Acts 9:1-18) and the people gathered in Cornelius' house (Acts 10:24-48) all experienced salvation without the necessity of baptism. In his sermon at Pentecost, Peter urged those who had repented and believed in Christ to be baptized, not that baptism was necessary for salvation but as a testimony that they had been saved (Acts 2:1-41).

Thus, baptism is symbolic and not sacramental. Baptists believe that the Bible teaches that baptism symbolizes that a person has been saved and is not a means of salvation. Baptism is not a means of channeling saving grace but rather is a way of testifying that saving grace has been experienced. It does not wash away sin but symbolizes the forgiveness of sin through faith in Christ. While baptism is not essential for salvation, it is a very important requirement for obedience to the Lord. Christ commanded his disciples to baptize (Matthew 28:19) and therefore baptism is a form of obedience to Jesus as Lord. Baptism is one way that a person declares, "Jesus is Lord."

What is Believer's Baptism?

What is believer's baptism? Does it have a purpose, since salvation is "by grace through faith" (Ephesians 2:8,9)?

Water baptism is obviously a picture of something, which has already taken place in the heart of the believer the moment he/she was justified (1 Pet. 3:21). Water baptism is the ordinance by which the repentant believer identifies with the death, burial, and resurrection of Jesus Christ.

You are "crucified" (standing upright in water), you are "buried" (immersed into the water), and you are "resurrected into life" (raised out of the water). Water baptism then, is a picture of spiritual baptism as defined in Romans 6:3-5 and 1 Corinthians 12:13. It is the outward testimony of the believer's inward faith. A sinner is saved the moment he places his faith in the Lord Jesus Christ and yields to His Lordship in obedience. Baptism is the first visible testimony to that believer being set apart from his sin and set apart to Christ and His glory.

There is a scriptural basis for Believer's Baptism. It pictures or proclaims four important things:

1.   Believer's Baptism provides the picture of the believer's death, burial, and resurrection with Christ. "Buried with Him in baptism, wherein also ye are risen with Him, through the faith of the operation of God, who hath raised Him from the dead." Colossians 2:12

1.   Believer's Baptism is the picture the death of our old life to sin, and our resurrection to walk in newness of life. "As Christ was raised up from the dead, by the glory of the Father, even so we also should walk in newness of life." Romans 6:4

1.   Believer's Baptism proclaims our faith in the Trinity of the Godhead. "Baptizing them in the Name of the Father, and of the Son, and of the Holy Ghost." Matthew 28:19

1.   Believer's Baptism pictures our "putting on" of Christ. "For ye are all the children of God by faith in Christ Jesus. For as many of you as have been baptized into Christ have put on Christ. Galatians 3:26,27

So then, Believer's Baptism is a picture of what transpired when you placed your faith and trust in the death, burial, and resurrection of Jesus Christ to save you from your sins (Romans 6:3-5). It does not atone for sin, as it cannot; only the blood of Christ cleanses us from sin (I John 1:7; Colossians 1:14).

Who may be baptized?

Now, let's look at who may be baptized. The Bible makes it clear that scriptural baptism is Believer's Baptism and thus baptism is open to any who believe.

1.   In Acts 2:41 we observe that they received the word, **AND THEN** they were baptized.

1.   In Acts 8:12,36,37 we find that they believed, **AND THEN** they were baptized.

1.   In Acts 10:43,44,47, it is plain to see that those who believed received the Holy Ghost, and THEN they were baptized. (Lost people do not receive the Holy Ghost).

When the Philippian jailer asked, "What must I do to be saved?" they said, "Believe on the Lord Jesus Christ, and thou shalt be saved...." (Acts 16:30-34). Paul did not tell him to be baptized to be saved. His baptism came **AFTER** his believing, which, again, portrays the scriptural standard. Who then may/should be baptized? According to the established Bible pattern, only those who have repented and yielded to the Lordship of Christ. Water baptism is NOT salvation, but obedience to a command by God concerning discipleship.

When and where should baptism be done?

When is the believer to be baptized? The Bible teaches that water baptism follows shortly after spiritual baptism (the new birth). Notice the example of Paul (Acts 9:18), Cornelius (Acts 10:43-48), and the Philippian Jailer (Acts 16:33).

You were placed into the body of Christ by spiritual baptism at the moment you were saved (Galatians 3:26-27). Now you follow the miracle of spiritual baptism with physical immersion into water, according to Acts 8:38; 10:47; 16:33. As to where a believer is to be baptized, the obvious answer is in the presence of other believers, the local church, as to when, it should be done as soon as your church can manage. The Lord Jesus Christ gave the local church the ordinance of water baptism (Matthew 28:18-20). An ordinance is a ceremony appointed by Christ to be administered in the local church as a visible type of the sacrifice of Christ on Calvary.

How is baptism practiced

HOW is a believer to be baptized? Immersion in water is the only scriptural method of baptism.

1.   In Matthew 3:13-16 and in Mark 1:9-10 we find that John the Baptist needed "much water" for baptism.

1.   In Acts 8:38-39 we are taught baptism by immersion.

1.   In Romans 6:3-6 we see that baptism must fulfill three pictures: death, burial and resurrection. It is also referred to as being "planted", and being raised. It is not difficult to see that the only mode of baptism, which fulfills all these pictures, is the immersion of the believer in water. Furthermore, scriptural expressions such as "much water" (John 3:23), and "down both into

the water" (Acts 8:38) are very conclusive evidence that water baptism is by immersion.

Why be baptized?

Obedience: Spiritual baptism is the Christian's identification with Christ (Colossians 2:12). This is why we should submit to water baptism.

Romans 6:3-5 teaches us that it is literally a picture of your death, burial and resurrection with Christ. It is your first act of obedience to God after salvation. WHY be baptized? Consider the following:

1.   Believer's Baptism pleases the Lord. When Jesus was baptized, God the Father said, "This is my beloved Son, in whom I am well pleased" (Matthew 3:17). When we follow the example of the Lord Jesus Christ we certainly please the Father.

1.   Scriptural baptism is a testimony to the world. Jesus said, "Whosoever therefore shall confess me before men, him will I confess also before my Father which is in heaven" (Matthew 10:32). Our baptism is a public testimony o f our faith in the Lord Jesus: Christ, and the way in which we identify ourselves with Christ in His death, burial and resurrection.

We understand and believe that **baptism is not a "sacrament" that imparts saving grace, but an ordinance.** We are not saved by baptism, but by faith in Jesus Christ and His blood…"cleanseth us from all sin" (1 John 1:7). Baptism is the outward symbol of what has already transpired in the heart of the one who has trusted the Lord Jesus Christ for full salvation.

The Lord's Table (Holy Communion)

There is a 2nd ordinance that is enjoined upon all believers, the The Lord's Supper also referred to as the Lord's Table or Holy Communion. The Lord's Supper, consisting of the elements --bread and the fruit of the vine-- is the symbol expressing our sharing the divine nature of our Lord Jesus Christ (2 Peter 1:4), a memorial of his suffering and death (1 Corinthians 11:26, and a prophecy of His second coming (1 Corinthians 11:26, and is enjoined on all believers "till He come!"

Let us focus on the teaching of the London Baptist Confession for a few moments:

1.   The supper of the Lord Jesus was instituted by him the same night wherein he was betrayed, to be observed in his churches, unto the end of the world, for the perpetual remembrance, and shewing forth the sacrifice of himself in his death, confirmation of the faith of believers in all the benefits thereof, their spiritual nourishment, and growth in him, their further engagement in, and to all duties which they owe to him; and to be a bond and pledge of their communion with him, and with each other. (1 Corinthians 11:23-26; 1 Corinthians 10:16, 17, 21)

There is no set mandate upon the Church as to how often we come to the Lord's Table that is found in Scripture and neither do I enjoin the church to a particular timetable. It is to the Elders to decide if weekly, monthly, etc. All believers are entitled to partake upon their conversion and, having professed faith, are encouraged to receive Holy Communion from the Elders in full view and fellowship with the Household of the Faithful during corporate worship.

1.   **In this ordinance Christ is not offered up to his Father, nor any real sacrifice made at all for remission of sin of the quick or dead, but only a memorial of that one offering up of himself by himself upon the cross, once for all; and a spiritual oblation of all possible praise unto God for the same. So that the popish sacrifice of the mass, as they call it, is most abominable, injurious to Christ's own sacrifice the alone propitiation for all the sins of the elect. (Hebrews 9:25, 26, 28; 1 Corinthians 11:24; Matthew 26:26, 27)**

1.   The Lord Jesus hath, in this ordinance, appointed his ministers to pray, and bless the elements of bread and wine, and thereby to set them apart from a common to a holy use, and to take and break the bread; to take the cup, and, they communicating also themselves, to give both to the communicants. (1 Corinthians 11:23-26, etc.)

1.   The denial of the cup to the people, worshipping the elements, the lifting them up, or carrying them about for adoration, and reserving them for any pretended religious use, are all contrary to the nature of this ordinance, and to the institution of Christ. (Matthew 26:26-28; Matthew 15:9; Exodus 20:4, 5)

1.   The outward elements in this ordinance, duly set apart to the use ordained by Christ, have such relation to him crucified, as that truly, although in terms used figuratively, they are sometimes called by the names of the things they represent, to wit, the body and blood of Christ, albeit, in substance and nature, they still remain truly and only bread and wine, as they were before. (1 Corinthians 11:27; 1 Corinthians 11:26-28)

1.   That doctrine which maintains a change of the substance of bread and wine, into the substance of Christ's body and blood, commonly called transubstantiation, by consecration of a priest, or by any other way, is repugnant not to Scripture alone, but even to common sense and reason, overthroweth the nature of the ordinance, and hath been, and is, the cause of manifold superstitions, yea, of gross idolatries. (Acts 3:21; Luke 24:6, 39; 1 Corinthians 11:24, 25)

1.   Worthy receivers, outwardly partaking of the visible elements in this ordinance, do then also inwardly by faith, really and indeed, yet not carnally and corporally, but spiritually receive, and feed upon Christ crucified, and all the benefits of his death; the body and blood of Christ being then not corporally or carnally, but spiritually present to the faith of believers in that ordinance, as the elements themselves are to their outward senses. (1 Corinthians 10:16; 1 Corinthians 11:23-26)

1.   All ignorant and ungodly persons, as they are unfit to enjoy communion with Christ, so are they unworthy of the Lord's table, and cannot, without great sin against him, while they remain such, partake of these holy

mysteries, or be admitted thereunto; yea, whosoever shall receive unworthily, are guilty of the body and blood of the Lord, eating and drinking judgment to themselves. (2 Corinthians 6:14, 15; 1 Corinthians 11:29; Matthew 7:6)

How should Holy Communion be administered and by whom?
Before we go any further, it is needful to remind that Holy Communion is a closed ceremony, meaning it should only be offered during the Corporate Worship to a believer that has submitted to Believers Baptism. Many of my Baptist Brethren will disagree with this. However, the command to be baptized is scriptural and disobedience to this command necessarily disqualifies from the observance of Communion.
It is appointed to ministers to bless the elements and to distribute among the faithful. Both offices, the Elders and the Deacons should be present in the service. Otherwise there is no set formula apart from scripture. The bread is to be blessed, broken, and eaten. Following this, the cup is to be blessed and drank.

This is our Thanksgiving Celebration in which we remember that Christ gave us the ultimate gift, Himself, so that we might be redeemed unto Him and enjoy fellowship for ever.

Lesson 8: Kingdom Come-The Doctrine of Last Days
This is where things can get a little prickly. Dispensationalists and adherents of Covenant Theology have very divergent viewpoints on eschatology.

In Classic Dispensationalism, there are seven dispensations and this lesson brings us to the final dispensation, Last Things/The Kingdom/Last Days. It is important to remember that Dispensationalism is a theology inferred from Scripture rather than an explicitly taught doctrine of God's Word. The value of Dispensationalism lies in its systematic view of history's different eras and the various ways in which the Ancient of Days interacts with His creation.

There are several components to Last Days, beginning with the Rapture

Rapture: The End Begins

What is the Rapture

The Rapture, also referred to as the Blessed Hope is an eschatological event and, in point of fact, is the event that begins the entirety of the End Times. Our official statement is thus: The resurrection of those who have fallen asleep in Christ and their translation together with those who are alive and remain unto the coming of the Lord is the imminent and blessed hope of the church. (1 Thessalonians 4:16,17 Romans 8:23 Titus 2:13 1 Corinthians 15:51,52)

This is the event where believers who are "alive and remain shall be caught up together…in the clouds to meet the Lord in the air" (1 Thessalonians 4:16-17). We would call this the First Resurrection, where each Christian receives his or her resurrected body, after which they will pass before the Bema Seat and then enter into the joy of their Lord. First to receive their new bodies are those who have died as Christians, and then, those who are "alive and remain."

1 Thessalonians 4:13-18
13 But I would not have you to be ignorant, brethren, concerning them which are asleep, that ye sorrow not, even as others which have no hope. (Being asleep, as the Apostle Paul uses here, is a euphemism. He simply means that they have died.)
14 For if we believe that Jesus died and rose again, even so them also which sleep in Jesus will God bring with him.
15 For this we say unto you by the word of the Lord, that we which are alive and remain unto the coming of the Lord shall not prevent them which are asleep.
16 For the Lord himself shall descend from heaven with a shout, with the voice of the archangel, and with the trump of God: and the dead in Christ shall rise first:
17 Then we which are alive and remain shall be caught up together with them in the clouds, to meet the Lord in the air: and so shall we ever be with the Lord.
18 Wherefore comfort one another with these words.

(The Second Resurrection occurs at the Great White Throne where the wicked dead and the remaining wicked who are living are resurrected to eternal fire.)

Take notice, I am telling you a secret. We shall not all die but we shall all be changed, in a moment, in the twinkling of an eye, at the last trumpet call. For the trumpet will sound and the dead will be raised imperishable, and we shall all be changed" (1 Corinthians 15:51-52).

Is it certain that there will be a Rapture?
Absolutely. All the prophecies related to the First Advent came to pass and so the prophecies related to the Second will happen as well.

When Will It Happen?
We cannot know that and anyone who says that they do know is a liar. We do know that the rapture will be instantaneous, in "the twinkling of an eye" (1 Corinthians 15:51-52). Scripture nowhere encourages us to try to determine the date of Jesus' return. Rather, we are to "keep watch, because we do not know on which day our Lord will come" (Matthew 24:42). We are to "be ready, because the Son of Man will come at an hour when we do not expect Him" (Matthew 24:44). In the eschatological Parable of the Talents, we are told by the Lord to "Occupy till I come" but what does that mean? It means that we must be about the work of spreading the message of the Gospel.

Exploring the Truth takes the position of a premillennial, pre-tribulational rapture of the church and we have been told that such a position is actually detrimental to the work of the Kingdom; I could not disagree more. If we truly believe that the Rapture of the Church is imminent, it should motivate us greatly. The true work of the Kingdom is to proclaim the Gospel of Jesus Christ and that He is coming soon.

The timing of the Rapture has sparked a great debate within Christianity as a whole. Will it occur before, during, or after the tribulation period? Will it occur before the Millennial Kingdom begins, after the Millennial Kingdom ends, or, perhaps, will there be no Millennial Kingdom at all? Since we take the position of a Premillennial, Pretribulational Rapture of the Church, we need to define our terms. The tribulation is a seven-year period that immediately precedes the return of Christ and the establishment of His millennial kingdom, which lasts for 1,000 years. The first 3 ½ years of the tribulation will be a time of peace and cooperation, and the second 3 ½ years of the tribulation will be a time of war and catastrophe. At the midpoint of the tribulation, the Antichrist will proclaim himself god and require worship from all people of the world. Many will bow down and worship the Antichrist, including taking his mark of worldwide registration. Some will refuse to worship the Antichrist and receive his mark, and many will be killed for this act of disobedience. The second half of the tribulation is referred to as the "Great Tribulation." There will be extraordinary catastrophes all over the world during this period. (For scriptural support, see Revelation 3:10, Matthew 24; Mark 13 and Luke 17).

Why do we take this position? In answering this question, it is important that we understand the culture of the day as well as the metaphor in play. In Revelation 19, we see the Marriage Supper of the Lamb referred to. This is noteworthy because it is the metaphor that we are to follow.

I had the privilege to sit under a Messianic Jewish Rabbi and he explained this as following the Paleo-Hebraic wedding. Let us look at that metaphor in regard to the Rapture and the rest of the End Times.

First, there is the Mohar (the Bride Price or Dowry). In the case of the Church, who is the Bride of Christ, the price was His own precious blood. Next, there is erusin, the betrothal. At the betrothal the woman was legally married, although she still remained in her father's house. She could not belong to another man unless she was divorced from her betrothed. The wedding meant only that the betrothed woman, accompanied by a colorful procession, was brought from her father's house to the house of her groom, and the legal tie with him was consummated. This is a beautiful picture of Sovereign Election; we are betrothed to Christ in the moment of our election and we can, legally, belong to no other.

The bride and groom would dwell in a place prepared for them by the groom:

John 14:2-3 (NASB)
2 In My Father's house are many dwelling places; if it were not so, I would have told you; for I go to prepare a place for you. 3 If I go and prepare a place for you, I will come again and receive you to Myself, that where I am, there you may be also.

Only the father could determine when the dwelling place was ready.

Matthew 24:36 (KJV)
36 But of that day and hour knoweth no man, no, not the angels of heaven, but my Father only. This would begin a period of separation.

At the end of the period of separation the groom would come to take his bride to live with him. The taking of the bride usually took place at night. The groom, best man and other male escorts would leave the groom's father's house and conduct a torch light procession to the home of the bride. Although the bride was expecting her groom to come for her, she did not know the exact time of his coming. As a result, the groom's arrival would be preceded by a shout. This shout would forewarn the bride to be prepared for the coming of the groom. (The shout of the Archangel in 1 Thessalonians)

After the groom received his bride together with her female attendants, the enlarged wedding party would return from the bride's home to the groom's father's house. Upon arrival there the wedding party would find that the wedding guests had assembled already.

Shortly after arrival the bride and groom would be escorted by the other members of the wedding party to the bridal chamber (Chuppah). Prior to entering the chamber, the bride remained veiled so that no one could see her face. While the groomsmen and bridesmaids would wait outside, the bride and groom would enter the bridal chamber alone. There in the privacy of that place they would enter into physical union for the first time, thereby consummating the marriage that had been covenanted earlier. After the marriage was consummated, the groom would announce the consummation to the other members of the wedding party waiting outside the chamber (John 3:29). These people would pass on the news of the marital union to the wedding guests. Upon receiving this good news, the wedding guests would feast and make merry for the next seven days. During the seven days of the wedding festivities, which were sometimes called "the seven days of the Chuppah," the bride remained hidden in the bridal chamber. At the conclusion of these seven days the groom would bring his bride out of the bridal chamber, now with her veil removed, so that all could see who his bride was.

In the same manner as the Jewish bridegroom came to the bride's home for the purpose of obtaining her through the establishment of a marriage covenant, so Jesus came to earth for the purpose of obtaining the Church through the establishment of a covenant. On the same night in which Jesus made His promise in John 14, He instituted communion (This is the Covenant sign of our betrothal to Him). As He passed the cup of wine to His disciples, He said: "This cup is the new covenant in my blood" (1 Cor. 11:25). This was His way of saying that He would establish a new covenant through the shedding of His blood on the cross. Parallel to the custom of the Jewish groom paying a price to purchase his bride, Jesus paid a price to purchase His bride, the Church. The price that He paid was His own life blood. It was because of this purchase price that Paul wrote the following to members of the Church: "know ye not that...ye are not your own? For ye are bought with a price: therefore, glorify God in your body, and your spirit, which are God's" (1 Cor. 6:19-20).

Analogous with the Jewish bride being declared to be sanctified or set apart exclusively for her groom once the marriage covenant was established, the Church has been declared to be sanctified or set apart exclusively for Christ (Eph. 5:25-27; 1Cor. 1:2; 6:11; Heb. 10:10; 13:12).

In the same way that a cup of wine served as a symbol of the marriage covenant through which the Jewish groom obtained his bride, so the cup of communion serves as the symbol of the covenant through which Christ has obtained the Church (1 Cor. 11:25).

Just as the Jewish groom left the home of his bride and returned to his father's house after the marriage covenant had been established, so Jesus left the earth, the home of the Church, and returned to His Father's house in heaven after He had established the new covenant and risen from the dead (John 6:62; 20:17). Corresponding with the period of separation between the Jewish groom and bride, Christ has remained separate from the Church for over 1900 years. The Church is now living in that period of separation.

Parallel to the custom of the Jewish groom preparing living accommodations for his bride in his father's house during the time of separation, Christ has been preparing living accommodations for the Church in His Father's house in heaven during His separation from His Bride (John 14:2).

In the same manner as the Jewish groom came to take his bride to live with him at the end of the period of separation, so Christ will come to take His Church to live with Him at the end of His period of separation from the Church (John 14:3).
Just as the taking of the Jewish bride was accomplished by a procession of the groom and male escorts from the groom's father's house to the home of the bride, so the taking of the Church will be accomplished by a procession of Christ and an angelic escort from Christ's Father's house in heaven to the home of the Church (1 Thess. 4:16).

Just as the Jewish bride was not knowing the exact time of the groom's coming for her, the Church does not know the exact time of Christ's coming for her.

In the same way that the Jewish groom's arrival was preceded by a shout, so Christ's arrival to take the Church will be preceded by a shout (1 Thess. 4:16).

Similar to the Jewish bride's return with the groom to his father's house after her departure from her home, the Church will return with Christ to His Father's house in heaven after she is snatched from the earth to meet Him in the air (1 Thess. 4:17; John 14:2-3). What will happen here taught using the Greek word harpazo, which means to catch away. In the connotation of harpazo, it is very similar to being caught by the collar and being drug away. It is at that point that we will experience the other word related to the Rapture, Paralambano, which is a taking to oneself. The Angelic Host will catch us out of this world (harpazo in Greek, rapturus in Latin and that is where the word rapture comes from) and will deliver us unto Jesus who, being the perfect groom will take us unto himself.

In the same manner as the Jewish wedding party found wedding guests assembled in the groom's father's house when they arrived, so Christ and the Church will find the souls of Old Testament saints assembled in heaven when they arrive. These souls will serve as the wedding guests. What a glorious event that will be!! The saints of old gathered together to witness the joining of the Prince of Heaven to His bride; can you even imagine and she is presented to Him in a robe of fine linen, white and pure and, in final glorification, the Bride reflects the radiant majesty of Jesus Christ?! This, beloved, is the reward we long for; not streets of gold, not gates fashioned from a single pearl, not mansions or crowns or anything else. The reward of our faithfulness is that we will be with Jesus and will enjoy His presence forever, in complete fellowship the way it was in the garden before the fall.

Parallel to the custom of the Jewish groom and bride entering into physical union after their arrival at the groom's father's house, thereby consummating the marriage that had been covenanted earlier, Christ and the Church will experience spiritual union after their arrival at His Father's house in heaven, thereby consummating their relationship that had been covenanted earlier.

Corresponding with the Jewish bride remaining hidden in the bridal chamber for a period of seven days after arrival at the groom's father's house, the Church will remain hidden for a period of seven after arrival at Christ's Father's house in heaven. While the seven-year Tribulation Period is taking place on the earth, the Church will be in heaven totally hidden from the sight of those living on the earth.
Just as the Jewish groom brought his bride out of the bridal chamber at the conclusion of the seven days with her veil removed, so that all could see who his bride was, so Christ will bring His Church out of heaven in His Second Coming at the conclusion of the seven-year Tribulation Period in full view of all who are alive, so that all can see who the true church is (Col. 3:4).

Beloved, can you see the majesty of this event? The ultimate groom is coming for His bride. The Crown Prince of Heaven, adorned in majesty, wearing glory for His garments is coming to take His bride home. We, the Church are that Bride and we are about to enter into the "7 days of the Chuppa" but for those left behind, they will be a time of terrible tribulation, one year for each day of the Marriage Supper…

In reality, the main debate on the Rapture is not what it's nature is, but when it will occur in relation to the tribulation. To summarize, the **pre-tribulation** view is that the rapture will happen before the tribulation period, and this is the position that we take; the **mid-tribulation** view is that the rapture will occur half-way through the tribulation period; and the **post-tribulation** view is that the rapture will occur at the end of the tribulation period.

Does the Timing Matter for Believers in Jesus Christ?

The pre-tribulation rapture is a wonderful hope for believers in Jesus Christ, which is why the Apostle tells us to comfort one another with those words.

That being said, when the Rapture actually happens is, to a point, ancillary. The key to our position in Christ, and to securing our home-going, is that we are justified by faith in Christ because of grace.

At a point following the Rapture we find...

Tribulation: The Wrath to Come

The Biblical Basis for The Tribulation
Does the Bible teach that there will be a Great Tribulation (also called the Time of Jacob's trouble? Does it teach that there will be an actual person who we know as the Antichrist? In short, Yes.

What are the Tribulation and Great Tribulation (gotquestions.org)?
The Tribulation is a future time period when the Lord will accomplish at least two aspects of His plan: 1) He will complete His discipline of the nation Israel (Daniel 9:24), and 2) He will judge the unbelieving, godless inhabitants of the earth (Revelation 6 - 18). The length of the Tribulation is seven years. This is determined by an understanding of the seventy weeks of Daniel (Daniel 9:24-27; also see the article on the Tribulation). The Great Tribulation is the last half of the Tribulation period, three and one-half years in length. It is distinguished from the Tribulation period because the Beast, or Antichrist, will be revealed, and the wrath of God will greatly intensify during this time. Thus, it is important at this point to emphasize that the Tribulation and the Great Tribulation are not synonymous terms. Within eschatology (the study of future things), the Tribulation refers to the full seven-year period while the "Great Tribulation" refers to the second half of the Tribulation.

It is Christ Himself who used the phrase "Great Tribulation" with reference to the last half of the Tribulation. In Matthew 24:21, Jesus says, "For then there will be a great tribulation, such as has not occurred since the beginning of the world until now, nor ever shall." In this verse Jesus is referring to the event of Matthew 24:15, which describes the revealing of the abomination of desolation, the man also known as the Antichrist. Also, Jesus in Matthew 24:29-30 states, "Immediately after the tribulation of those days . . . the Son of Man will appear in the sky, and then all the tribes of the earth will mourn, and they will see the Son of Man coming on the clouds of the sky with power and great glory." In this passage, Jesus defines the Great Tribulation (v.21) as beginning with the revealing of the abomination of desolation (v.15) and ending with Christ's second coming (v.30).

Other passages that refer to the Great Tribulation are Daniel 12:1b, which says, "And there will be a time of distress such as never occurred since there was a nation until that time." It seems that Jesus was quoting this verse when He spoke the words recorded in Matthew 24:21. Also referring to the Great Tribulation is Jeremiah 30:7, "Alas! for that day is great, There is none like it; And it is the time of Jacob's distress, But he will be saved from it." The phrase "Jacob's distress" refers to the nation of Israel, which will experience persecution and natural disasters such as have never before been seen.

Considering the information Christ gave us in Matthew 24:15-30, it is easy to conclude that the beginning of the Great Tribulation has much to do with the abomination of desolation, an action of the Antichrist. In Daniel 9:26-27, we find that this man will make a "covenant" (a peace pact) with the world for seven years (one "week"; again, see the article on the Tribulation). Halfway through the seven-year period—"in the middle of the week"—we are told this man will break the covenant he made, stopping sacrifice and grain offering, which specifically refers to his actions in the rebuilt temple of the future. Revelation 13:1-10 gives even more detail concerning the Beast's actions, and just as important, it also verifies the length of time he will be in power. Revelation 13:5 says he will be in power for 42 months, which is three and one-half years, the length of the Great Tribulation.

Revelation offers us the most information about the Great Tribulation. From Revelation 13 when the Beast is revealed until Christ returns in Revelation 19, we are given a picture of God's wrath on the earth because of unbelief and rebellion (Revelation 16-18). It is also a picture of how God disciplines and at the same time protects His people Israel (Revelation 14:1-5) until He keeps His promise to Israel by establishing an earthly kingdom (Revelation 20:4-6).

The first mention of the Tribulation in the Bible is found in Deuteronomy 4:27-30. Before the Children of Israel entered the Promised Land, Moses warned them that if they were unfaithful to God, they would be scattered among the nations. He then prophesied that "in the latter days" they would come under "distress," and the result would be their "return to the Lord."

Centuries later, Jeremiah used the same terminology when he referred to the Tribulation. He called it "the time of Jacob's Trouble" (Jeremiah 30:7). Similarly, Daniel called it "the time of trouble," and he prophesied it would be the worst period of trouble in the history of the Jewish people (Daniel 12:1). Malachi stated it would be a time of refining for the Jews, as when silver is purified by fire (Malachi 3:1-4). And Zechariah used the same imagery when he prophesied that two-thirds of the Jewish people will perish during this time. Of the remnant remaining, he wrote, "I [the Lord] will bring the third part through the fire [and] refine them as silver is refined..." (Zechariah 13:8-9). Incidentally, it is this remnant that prompts us to teach that all of Israel will be saved.

All Israel Will Be Saved During the Tribulation

That all Israel will be saved is a logical possibility that we can readily draw from the text.

In two of the sets of judgments, we see the unmitigated death and destruction that the Holy God allows to be unleashed on a Christ Rejecting world. What we do not see, in Revelation, is how many of those who are killed are part of Israel and as a consequence we do not know how many Israelites are left alive to be saved. We can, then, infer that the salvation of Israel is logically possible. As to probability, bear with me...

SEALS
Rev.6:3-2nd Seal: Wars on earth
Rev.6:7-4th Seal: Death released. 1/4 of the worlds population to die by plagues, disease, and beasts of the earth
Rev.6:9-5th Seal: Persecution and mass killing of God's people worldwide
Rev.6:12-6th Seal: Massive earthquake wrath of God.

TRUMPETS
Rev.9:13-6th Trumpet: demons released and 200 million army kills 1/3 of the world's population.

Some points from the Revelation Teaching Series by another of my mentors "shall be saved" ...salvation by faith in Jesus Christ vs works
1.   Genesis 15:6
1.   Habakkuk 2:4
1.   Romans 4:9 – 5:1
1.   Romans 9:24-26
1.   Galatians 3:16-29

"all Israel"
1.   Romans 2:25-29
1.   Romans 9:6b
1.   Romans 9:27
1.   Ezekiel 20:5, 8, 13, 16-17, 33-44

When will God rule over Israel...when will God be Israel's King?
When will Israel pollute His name no more?

When will Israel be sanctified before the Gentile nations?
When will Israel know that Jesus Christ is Lord?
When will Israel loathe themselves and their tawdry history?
When will the Lord purge Israel of the rebels/unbelievers?
During the 70th Week of Daniel (Dan 9:24)

1.   Ezekiel 36:16-31
1.   Zechariah 13:8-9
1.   Romans 11:25-29

"All Israel" are those who believe Jesus is the Christ, the Son of the Living God, their King and Savior

Dr. MacArthur points out that "all Israel" means all of those members of the nation of Israel that survive the Time of Jacob's Trouble/Great Tribulation.
Romans 11:17- only some branches are broken off, so a believing remnant are being preserved unto/until salvation.

Additional from Dr. MacArthur
Before **all Israel** is **saved,** its unbelieving, ungodly members will be separated out by God's inerrant hand of judgment. Ezekiel makes that truth vividly clear:

"As I live," declares the Lord God, "surely with a mighty hand and with an outstretched arm and with wrath poured out, I shall be king over you. And I shall bring you out from the peoples and gather you from the lands where you are scattered, with a mighty hand and with an outstretched arm and with wrath poured out; and I shall bring you into the wilderness of the peoples, and there I shall enter into judgment with you face to face. As I entered into judgment with your fathers in the wilderness of the land of Egypt, so I will enter into judgment with you," declares the Lord God. "And I shall make you pass under the rod, and I shall bring you into the bond of the covenant; and I shall purge from you the rebels and those who transgress against Me; I shall bring them out of the land where they sojourn, but they will not enter the land of Israel. Thus you will know that I am the Lord." (Ezek. 20:33–38, emphasis added; cf. Dan. 12:10; Zech. 13:8–9)

Those who hear the preaching of the 144,000 (Rev. 7:1–8; 14:1–5), of other converts (7:9), of the two witnesses (11:3–13), and of the angel (14:6), and thus safely pass under God's rod of judgment will then comprise all Israel, which—in fulfillment of God's sovereign and irrevocable promise—will be completely a nation of believers who are ready for the kingdom of the Messiah Jesus.

"Behold, days are coming," declares the Lord, "when I will make a new covenant with the house of Israel and with the house of Judah, not like the covenant which I made with their fathers in the day I took them by the hand to bring them out of the land of Egypt, My covenant which they broke, although I was a husband to them," declares the Lord. "But this is the covenant which I will make with the house of Israel after those days," declares the Lord, "I will put My law within them, and on their heart I will write it; and I will be their God, and they shall be My people. And they shall not teach again, each man his neighbor and each man his brother, saying, 'Know the Lord,' for they shall all know Me, from the least of them to the greatest of them," declares the Lord, "for I will forgive their iniquity, and their sin I will remember no more." (Jer. 31:31–34; cf. 32:38)

God's control of history is irrefutable evidence of His sovereignty. And as surely as He cut off unbelieving Israel from His tree of salvation, just as surely will He graft believing Israel back in—a nation completely restored and completely saved.

Most importantly, the reason why, at some point, the entirety of Israel looks upon Him whom they pierced, mourns, and turns to Christ is the fact that God does not change

Malachi 3:6
I, the Lord, do not change

Hosea 2:14-20
14"Therefore, behold, I will allure her, and bring her into the wilderness, and speak tenderly to her. **15**And there I will give her her vineyards and make the Valley of Achore a door of hope. And there she shall answer as in the days of her youth, as at the time when she came out of the land of Egypt. **16**"And in that day, declares the LORD, you will call me 'My Husband,' and no longer will you call me 'My Baal.' **17**For I will remove the names of the Baals from her mouth, and they shall be remembered by name no more. **18**And I will make for them a covenant on that day with the beasts of the field, the birds of the heavens, and the creeping things of the ground. And I will abolish the bow, the sword, and war from the land, and I will make you lie down in safety. **19**And I will betroth you to me forever. I will betroth you to me in righteousness and in justice, in steadfast love and in mercy. **20** I will betroth you to me in faithfulness. And you shall know the LORD.

1 Samuel 15:29
29 "And also the Glory of Israel will not lie or change His mind; for He is not a man that He should change His mind"

Psalm 102:12 & 25-28

12 But Thou, O LORD dost abide forever; And Thy name to all generations. . .
25 Of old Thou didst found the earth; And the heavens are the work of Thy
hands. 26 Even they will perish, but Thou dost endure; And all of them will
wear out like a garment; Like clothing Thou wilt change them, and they will
be changed. 27 But Thou art the same, And Thy years will not come to an end.
28 The children of Thy servants will continue, and their descendants will be
established before Thee"

The Scope of Tribulation

The House of Israel will not be the only ones to suffer during this period of
unparalleled trouble. The Bible makes it clear that all the nations of the world
will experience catastrophic calamities.

Isaiah calls it "a day of reckoning" for all the nations of the world (Isaiah 2:10-
17). Zephaniah says "all the earth will be devoured in the fire of God's
jealousy" (Zephaniah 1:18). The Psalmist Asaph put it this way: "A cup is in
the hand of the Lord, and the wine foams… surely, all the wicked of the earth
must drain and drink down its dregs" (Psalm 75:8).

How long will this be?

The prophet Daniel defined the length of the Tribulation. He said God would
accomplish all His purposes for the Jewish people during a period of 70 weeks
of years (490 years). Sixty-nine of those weeks of years (483 years) would
lead up to the death of the Messiah. The final week of years would occur at the
end of the age, right before the return of the Messiah (Daniel 9:24-27). This
concluding week of years (7 years) corresponds to the Tribulation for, as
Daniel put it, it will mark the time when "the prince who is to come" will
"make desolate" — a reference to the Antichrist.

The timing established by Daniel is confirmed in the book of Revelation where
the Tribulation is divided into two periods of 3 1/2 years each (Revelation
11:3,7 and 13:5). The dividing point between the two halves of the Tribulation
will occur when the Antichrist reveals himself by entering the rebuilt Temple
in Jerusalem, stopping the sacrifices, and declaring himself to be god
(Matthew 24:15; 2 Thessalonians 2:3-4; and Revelation 13:5-6).

When does this happen?

When will this terrible period begin? The Bible says in general terms that it
will start after the Jews have been re-gathered and have been re-established in
their homeland and in their sacred city of Jerusalem.

Specifically, the Bible says it will begin at a time when all the world comes together against Israel over the issue of who will control the city of Jerusalem (Zechariah 12:2-3). Of course, this means that, currently, we are on the very threshold of the Tribulation today as we witness the United Nations, the European Union, the Vatican, and the Arab nations demanding that the Jews surrender their sovereignty over Jerusalem. Ultimately, this will not happen as God Himself will rise up to defend Israel, His beloved.

The specific event that will mark the seven year count down of the Tribulation will be the signing of a peace treaty between Israel and her Arab enemies — a treaty that will allow the Jews to rebuild their Temple (Daniel 9:27).

The Nature
The unparalleled horror of the Tribulation is spelled out in detail in both Tanakh and the New Testament. Isaiah wrote that it will be a day of "terror of the Lord" when "the pride of men will be abased" (Isaiah 2:10,17,19). Zephaniah proclaimed that it will be a "day of wrath," "a day of trouble and distress," and "a day of destruction and desolation" (Zephaniah 1:15). Men will stumble around like they are blind and "their blood will be poured out like dust" (Zephaniah 1:17).

This dismal picture is echoed in the New Testament. Jesus said it will be a time of tribulation "such as has not occurred since the beginning of the world until now, nor ever shall" (Matthew 24:21). In fact, Jesus said it will be so terrible that if it were not stopped at the end of seven years, it would result in the destruction of all life (Matthew 24:22). The Apostle John states that the chaos will be so great that the leaders of the world will crawl into caves and cry out for the rocks of the mountains to fall upon them (Revelation 6:15-16).

The Millennial Kingdom and, later the End of Days, are the final components of the 7th Dispensation, Last Things (Revelation 20:1-10).

Stewards: The resurrected Old Testament saints, the glorified Church, and survivors of the Tribulation and their descendants
The Period: From the Second Coming of Jesus Christ until the final rebellion, a period of one thousand years
Responsibility: To be obedient, remain undefiled, and worship the Lord Jesus (Isaiah 11:3-5; Zechariah 14:9)
Failure: After Satan is loosed from the Abyss, sinful man rebels one more time (Revelation 20:7-9)
Judgment: Fire from God; the Great White Throne Judgment (Revelation 20:9-15)

Grace: Jesus Christ restores creation and rules righteously in Israel, with all saints assisting (Isaiah 11:1-5; Matthew 25:31-46; Revelation 20)

The Millennial Kingdom will be a time characterized by peace (Isaiah 11:6-7; Micah 4:3), justice (Isaiah 11:3-4), unity (Isaiah 11:10), abundance (Isaiah 35:1-2), healing (Isaiah 35:5-6), righteousness (Isaiah 35:8), joy (Isaiah 55:12), and the physical presence of Christ (Isaiah 16:5). Satan will be bound in the Abyss during this period (Revelation 20:1-3). Messiah Jesus will be the benevolent dictator ruling over the whole world (Isaiah 9:6-7; 11). The resurrected saints of all times will participate in the management of the government (Revelation 20:4-6).

The Millennial Kingdom is measurable and comes after the Kingdom of God (embodied in Jesus Christ) came to man during the dispensation of Grace. On Jesus' first visit to the earth, He brought grace; at His Second Coming He will execute justice and usher in the Millennium. Jesus mentioned His glorious return at His trial before the Sanhedrin (Mark 14:62), and He was referring to the Millennial Kingdom when He taught His disciples to pray, "Thy kingdom come" (Matthew 6:10, KJV).

The rebellion at the end of the Millennial Kingdom seems almost incredible. Mankind will have been living in a perfect environment with every need cared for, overseen by a truly just government (Isaiah 11:1-5), yet they still try to do better. Man simply cannot maintain the perfection that God requires. Mankind follows Satan any chance he gets.

At the end of the Millennium, the final rebellion is crushed, and Satan will be cast into the lake of fire (Revelation 20:10). Then comes the Great White Throne Judgment where all the unrighteous of all of the dispensations will be judged according to their works and also cast into the lake of fire (Revelation 20:11-15).

After the final judgment, God and His people live forever in the New Jerusalem on a new earth with a new heaven (Revelation 21). God's plan of redemption will have been completely realized, and the redeemed will know God and enjoy Him forever."

There are 3 dominant views: Premillennialism, Postmillennialism, and A-millennialism. In *pre-millennialism*, Jesus returns *before* his thousand-year reign on earth. In *postmillennialism*, Jesus returns *after* an earthly golden age. In *a-millennialism*, the millennium is a *symbolic* time frame between Jesus' ascension and his return, when deceased believers reign with Christ in heaven. We will treat those a little more below.

Postmillennialism

Definition:
The postmillennialist believes that the millennium is an and not necessarily a literal thousand years during which Christ will reign over the earth, not from a literal and earthly throne, *but through the gradual increase of the Gospel and its power to change lives (emphasis mine)*. After this gradual Christianization of the world, Christ will return and immediately usher the church into their eternal state after judging the wicked. This is called postmillennialism because, by its view, Christ will return after the millennium.

Features and Distinctions:
1. Favored method of interpretation: covenant-historical.
1. Israel and the church: the church is the fulfillment of Israel.
1. Kingdom of God: a spiritual entity experienced on earth through the Christianizing affect of the Gospel.
1. The Millennium is viewed as a Golden Age previous to Christ's second advent during which Christ will virtually rule over the whole earth through an unprecedented spread of the Gospel; the large majority of people will be Christian.

Miscellaneous:
1. Higher degrees of interpreting First Century events in the light of prophecy; preterism often goes hand-in-hand with postmillennialism.
1. Of the several versions of postmillennial eschatology, the reconstructionist's seems to be gaining the most popularity in the world today.
1. Major proponents: Rousas J. Rushdoony, Greg L. Bahnsen, Kenneth L. Gentry Jr., David Chilton, and Gary North.

Synopsis:
There are several different versions of postmillennialism, but one of the views gaining the most popularity, is that of the theonomists. Generally speaking, the postmillennial theonomist viewpoint holds to a partial-preterist interpretation of Revelation and the various judgment prophecies in the Gospels, believing that the majority of those prophecies were fulfilled in 70 A.D. at the destruction of the temple in Jerusalem.

The postmillennialist sees the millennial kingdom as the fulfillment of God's promise to Abraham that he would become "a great nation" and that "all peoples on earth would be blessed" through him (Genesis 12:2-3). This holy reign will come about via gradual conversion (rather than pre-millennialism's cataclysmic Christological advent) through the spread of the Gospel — this incremental progress is drawn from many pictures found throughout Scripture (e.g., Deuteronomy 7:22 and Ezekiel 47:1-12).

Postmillennial optimism is also nurtured through many of prophetic psalmody. The Psalms often speak of all nations fearing Him, salvation being known among all nations, the ends of the earth fearing Him, *et cetera* (e.g., Psalm 2:1-12; Psalm 22:27; Psalm 67:2, Psalm 67:7; Psalm 102:15; Psalm 110:1). Another passage that well feeds this earthly optimism is Isaiah 2:2-3 in which the nations will stream to the righteousness of God.

In light of current world events, I must reject the idea that the preaching of the Gospel is ushering in any kind of "Golden Age" for the church. Instead, it is my considered opinion that we are living in a time of unmatched wickedness. The advent of social media has enabled all manner of wickedness to spread like an insipid virus throughout the souls of mankind.

Some would ask, "Can't social media be used to usher in the Kingdom?" Of course it could but it is not. Many of the largest and most influential "ministries" belong to false teachers and I find that to be indicative of the problem.

I do not, presently, see any indication that the world is becoming more Christ-like, holy, peaceful, or prosperous.

Amillennialism

Definition:
The amillennialist believes that the Kingdom of God was inaugurated at Christ's resurrection (sometimes called "inaugurated millennialism") at which point he gained victory over both Satan and the Curse. Christ is even now reigning at the right hand of the Father over His church. After this present age has ended, Christ will return and immediately usher the church into their eternal state after judging the wicked. The term "amillennialism" is actually a misnomer for it implies that Revelation 20:1-6 is ignored; in fact, the amillennialist's hermeneutic interprets it (and in fact, much of apocalyptic literature) non-literally.

Features and Distinctions:
1.   Favored method of interpretation: redemptive-historical.
1.   Israel and the church: The church is the eschatological fulfillment of Israel.
1.   Kingdom of God: a spiritual reality that all Christians partake in and that is seen presently by faith, but will be grasped by sight at the consummation.

1.   The Rapture: The saints, living and dead, shall meet the Lord in the clouds and immediately proceed to judge the nations with Christ and then follow Him into their eternal state.

1.   The Millennium: inaugurated with Christ's resurrection. In an "already/not yet" sense, Christ already reigns over all and is already victorious over Satan.

Miscellaneous:

1.   Higher degrees of interpreting prophecy in light of Christ's advent, death, resurrection, and glorification.

1.   Relies heavily on a two-age theology.

1.   Major proponents: Meredith Kline, Richard Gaffin, Robert B. Strimple, Gregory K. Beale, and John Murray.

Synopsis:
Eschatology is the study of the eschaton; the eschaton is equated with "last things." While other views focus on the final days of humankind on earth, amillennialism sees "the last things" as having been initiated at Christ's resurrection and so, being applicable from the earliest days of the Christian church (cf. Acts 2:16-21; 1 Corinthians 10:11; Hebrews 1:1-2; and 1 Peter 1:20). The amillennialist perspective sees the whole of God's redemptive revelation as twofold - promise and fulfillment; it also emphasizes that a strict-literal interpretation of Old Testament is not necessarily the most accurate way of determining what the text means.

The amillennial perspective emphasizes that the coming of the Kingdom of God is a two-part event. The first portion dawned at Christ's first advent (John the Baptist proclaimed at this time, "The kingdom of heaven is at hand" — Matthew 3:2). At the cross, Christ won final victory over death and Satan. And then He ascended to reign upon the throne of David forever (Luke 1:32-33; Acts 2:30-31). Now because we "look not at the things which are seen, but at the things which are not seen; for the things which are seen are temporal, but the things which are not seen are eternal" (2 Corinthians 4:18) — because of this, the amillennialist sees the final things already accomplished, though not yet seen by sight, but by faith (2 Corinthians 5:7).

An important note is the amilleniallist's view of the church in this world: a role of suffering. The Christian will be hated by all, just as was Christ (Matthew 10:22), for a servant is not greater than his master. Seeing this as the church's role on earth — to suffer as did Christ — the amillenialist can hold no hope for an earthly exaltation and longs for the fulfillment of the second stage of the coming of the Kingdom.

This second stage of the amillennial perspective is the final consummation of all the heavenly promises. The Christian will no longer see by faith alone, but by sight. All the shadowy things will pass away and our eternal reign with Christ will begin. The amillennialist, expecting no earthly glory for the church, places all his hope on this heavenly glory.

Of course Christ is victorious over Satan. That being said, If Satan is bound, I think that he probably did not get that memo. 2 Thessalonians 2:6 mentions a "restrainer" that many have identified as the spirit filled church. The context of the text does not really allow for that but, at the same time, it is evident that there is a direct Agent restraining the evil that is in the world. Said Agent, is the Holy Spirit. How do I come to this?

By mere elimination, the Holy Spirit must be the restrainer. All other possibilities fall far short of meeting the requirements of one who is to hold in check the forces of evil until the manifestation of Antichrist. Some of the alternate suggestions are out of harmony with the basic text itself.

The Wicked One is a personality, and his operations include the realm of the spiritual. The restrainer must likewise be a personality and of a spiritual order, to resist the wiles of the Devil and to hold Antichrist in check until the time of his revealing. Mere agencies or impersonal spiritual forces would be inadequate. Moreover, the masculine gender of II Thessalonians 2:7 requires the restrainer to be a person.

To believe all that is to be accomplished, the restrainer must be a member of the Godhead. Of necessity He must be stronger than the Man of Sin, and stronger than Satan. In order to restrain evil down through the course of the age, the restrainer must be eternal, for Satan and his workers of iniquity have made their influence felt throughout the entire history of the Church. Likewise, the sphere of sin is the whole world, making it imperative that the restrainer be one who is not limited by time or space. Such a one is the Holy Spirit of God, for He is omnipotent, eternal, and omnipresent throughout the universe, and therefore preeminently qualified to hold in check all of the Satanic forces of darkness.

I will not go so far as to say that He is using the true church to restrain evil though it is possible; His methodology is somewhat of a mystery as it is not directly revealed in Scripture.

What is certain, though, is that while Satan is not currently bound, he certainly is severely restrained by whatever method it is that the Holy Spirit is using.

Historical Premillennialism

Definition:
Historical premillennialists place the return of Christ just before the millennium and just after a time of great apostasy and tribulation. After the millennium, Satan will be loosed and Gog and Magog will rise against the kingdom of God; this will be immediately followed by the final judgment. While similar in some respects to the dispensational variety (in that they hold to Christ's return being previous the establishment of a thousand-year earthly reign), historical premillennialism differs in significant ways (notably in their method of interpreting Scripture).

Features and Distinctions:
1. Favored method of interpretation: grammatico-historical.
1. Israel and the church: The church is the fulfillment of Israel.
1. Kingdom of God: present through the Spirit since Pentecost - to be experienced by sight during the millennium after Christ's return.
1. The Rapture: The saints, living and dead, shall meet the Lord in the clouds immediately preceding the millennial reign.
1. The Millennium: Christ will return to institute a thousand-year reign on earth. The Millennium will see the re-establishment of temple worship and sacrifice as a remembrance of Christ's sacrifice.
1. Major proponents: George Eldon Ladd, Walter Martin, John Warwick Montgomery, and Theodore Zahn.

Synopsis:

The historical premillennialist's view interprets some prophecy in Scripture as having literal fulfillment while others demand a semi-symbolic fulfillment. As a case in point, the seal judgments (Revelation 6) are viewed as having fulfillment in the forces in history (rather than in future powers) by which God works out his redemptive and judicial purposes leading up to the end.

Rather than the belief of an imminent return of Christ, it is held that a number of historical events (e.g., the rise of the Beast and the False Prophet) must take place before Christ's Second Coming. This Second Coming will be accompanied by the resurrection and rapture of the saints (1 Thessalonians 4:15-18); this will inaugurate the millennial reign of Christ. The Jewish nation, while being perfectly able to join the church in the belief of a true faith in Christ, has no distinct redemptive plan as they would in the dispensational perspective. The duration of the millennial kingdom (Revelation 20:1-6) is unsure: literal or metaphorical.

Dispensational Premillenialism

Definition:
Dispensational premillennialists hold that Christ will come before a seven-year period of intense tribulation to take His church (living and dead) into heaven. After this period of fulfillment of divine wrath, He shall then return to rule from a holy city (*i.e.*, the New Jerusalem) over the earthly nations for one thousand years. After these thousand years, Satan, who was bound up during Christ's earthly reign, will be loosed to deceive the nations, gather an army of the deceived, and take up to battle against the Lord. This battle will end in both the judgment of the wicked and Satan and the entrance into the eternal state of glory by the righteous. This view is called premillenialism because it places the return of Christ before the millennium and it is called dispensational because it is founded in the doctrines of **dispensationalism**.

Features and Distinctions:
1. Favored method of interpretation: strict literal.
1. Israel and the church: views church and Israel as two distinct identities with two individual redemptive plans.
1. The **rapture** of the Church: The church is raptured before a seven-year tribulation (the seventieth week of Daniel - Daniel 9:24-27). This tribulational period contains the reign of the AntiChrist.
1. Millennium: Christ will return at the end of the great tribulation to institute a thousand-year rule from a holy city (the New Jerusalem). Those who come to believe in Christ during the seventieth week of Daniel (including the 144,000 Jews) and survive will go on to populate the earth during this time. Those who were raptured or raised previous to the tribulational period will reign with Christ over the millennial population.

Miscellaneous:
1. Higher degrees of interpreting present-day events in the light of end-times prophecy.
1. The Millennium will see the re-establishment of temple worship and sacrifice as a remembrance of Christ's sacrifice.
1. From the millennium-ending "white throne" judgment (by which Satan and all unbelievers will be thrown into the lake of fire) Christ and all saints will proceed into eternal glory.
1. Major proponents: John Walvoord, Charles Ryrie, Louis Sperry Chafer, J. Dwight Pentecost, Norman Geisler, Charles Stanley, John MacArthur, David Jeremiah, Chuck Smith, and Chuck Missler.

Synopsis:

A strictly literal hermeneutic is foundational to the dispensational premillenialist viewpoint. Interpreting Scripture in this manner will in fact demand such perspectives unique to dispensationalism as:
1.   an earthly kingdom of God from which Christ will reign
1.   a future redemptive plan for national Israel
1.   a seven year period of great tribulation
1.   the rejection of prophetic idiom

Dispensational premillennialism holds that a seven-year tribulation (forseen in Daniel 9:27) will precede a thousand-year period (Revelation 20:1-6) during which time, Christ will reign on the throne of David (Luke 1:32).

Immediately previous to the time of great tribulation, all the dead saints will rise from their graves and all the living members of the church shall be caught up with them to meet Christ in the clouds (1 Corinthians 15:51-52; 1 Thessalonians 4:15-17); this is known as "the rapture." During this time of tribulation, there will be three-and-a-half years of world peace under an AntiChrist figure (Daniel 7:8; Revelation 13:1-8) who will establish a world-church (Revelation 17:1-15), followed by three-and-a-half years of greater suffering (Revelation 6-18). At the end of this period, Christ will return (Matthew 24:27-31; Revelation 19:11-21), judge the world (Ezekiel 20:33-38; Matthew 25:31; Jude 1:14-15), bind Satan for one thousand years (Revelation 20:1-3), and raise the Old Testament and tribulation saints from the dead (Daniel 12:2; Revelation 20:4).

At this time, the millennial reign will begin and Christ will reign politically over the earth at this time from His capital in Jerusalem (Isaiah 2:3). Throughout His reign, there will be no war (Isaiah 2:4) and even the natures of animals will dwell in harmony (Isaiah 11:6-9). At the end of this era of peace, Satan will be released and instigate a colossal (but futile) rebellion against God (Revelation 20:7-9). After this fated battle, Satan and the wicked are cast into the lake of fire (Revelation 20:10), while the righteous proceed into their eternal state in the realm of the new heaven and the new earth (Revelation 21:1).

Those in the amillennial camp, often, accuse Dispensationalist of teaching a "secret" rapture. I must confess that I find that idea not just a little odd but also just a bit absurd. There is nothing, at all, in the text (1 Thessalonians 4) that even remotely portends to the rapture being a secret. I suspect, instead, that the entire world will hear the trumpet blow but will not truly understand what is happening. Further, it is also a logical possibility that the entire world will hear the shout from heaven and not understand that either.

As to our stance on the Kingdom, many Covenant Theologians will accuse those of us who are dispensational of teaching two different kingdoms; this is not quite correct. Prophecy almost always has an already but not yet component to it. The Kingdom most certainly began when Jesus began His earthly ministry; He even said that the Kingdom of God was at hand and you, frankly, do not get much more clear than that. However, we see in Acts 1:6 that the disciples fully expected Jesus to restore a literal, physical kingdom to Israel. If the amillennialists were actually correct, it would mean that the disciples' question was in vain.

Let us turn to Dr. MacArthur's excellent lesson, Sovereign Election, Israel and Eschatology. I will quote him at length in dealing with amillennialism vs dispensationalism...

Were the Jews in Jesus' day Amill? No. Emil Schurer's helpful study of Jewish eschatology in the day of Jesus published in 1880 by TT&T Clark in Edinburgh--a new edition of it out in 1998 by Hendrickson Publishing --he does a great job of studying the Jewish Messianic eschatological mindset at the time of Jesus. Schurer is his name, S-c-h-u-r-e-r. They believed that the Messiah was coming, preceded by a time of trouble. They believed that before Messiah, Elijah the prophet would come. They believed that when Messiah came, He would be the personal Son of David, He would have special powers to set up His kingdom, and all Abrahamic covenant and Davidic covenant promises would be fulfilled. They also believed that Israel would repent and be saved at the coming of Messiah. They believed the kingdom would be established in Israel with Jerusalem at the center and would extend across the world. They believed that peace and righteousness would dominate the world, all people would worship the Messiah, there would be no war--only gladness and health. They believed in a re-instituted temple worship, and the fulfillment of the covenants included the renovation of the world, a general resurrection, final judgment and after that the eternal state. That's Jewish pre-New Testament eschatology. Dead on target. That's what Zacharias the priestly father of John the Baptist believed. Read Zacharias' great benedictus in Luke 1:67 to the end of the chapter, and what is he saying? Every single phrase that is in that comes from an Old Testament text on the Abrahamic covenant, the Davidic covenant, or the New Covenant. Every single one of them. He knew what was happening. The covenants were to be fulfilled.
Was Jesus an Amillennialist? This matters. Right? Was Jesus an Amillennialist? Turn to Acts 1. Acts 1. This has just been sitting there for a long time, by the way, like all the rest of the Scripture, and I don't know if we always look closely at these things. This is post-Resurrection, "[The] first account," verse 1, "I propose to Theophilus about all that Jesus began to do and teach until the day when He was taken up after He had by the Holy Spirit given orders to the apostles whom He had chosen." There is that election

again. So, he had spent time before His ascension with the apostles. Now verse 3, "To these He also presented Himself alive after His suffering by many convincing proofs appearing to them over a period of forty days." Literally appearing to them over forty days. It must have been intense. Can you imagine the level of teaching a resurrected Jesus would give His own over a forty-day period? What kind of a seminary education would that be? And what was He talking about? "...speaking of the things concerning the kingdom of God." Oh, this is perfect. This is perfect! For forty days He talked about the kingdom of God. This is His moment. If Jesus is an Amill, this is where He has to tell them. Their apostasy--that's a given. Their rejection of the Messiah--that's a given. The execution of the Messiah--that's a given. This is the perfect place for Jesus to launch Amillennialism. Go down to verse 6, "So when they had come together, they were asking Him saying, 'Lord, is it at this time you are restoring the kingdom to Israel?'" Now, what do you think He said? "Where did you get such a stupid idea? Where did you ever come up with that concept? Haven't you been listening for forty days?" "I'm an Amillennialist." "What a bizarre thought--that I am going to restore the kingdom to Israel!" "You don't listen." This is it. If Jesus is Amill, this is His moment! He's got to say, "No, the Church is the new Israel." Yeah. Is this the time the Father is going to restore..., according to Jewish sources the technical eschatological term for the end time. They were using a term that was a part of their eschatology. Is this the end time when You are restoring the kingdom to Israel? Forty days of instruction on the kingdom, and they knew one thing for sure, the kingdom for Israel was still coming. And all they wanted to know was, what's the question? WHEN? That's all. And He said to them, "It's not for you to know the times or seasons." You can't know timing. He didn't say "Wait, wait, wait, there isn't going to be a kingdom." He said, "It's not for you to know times and seasons". By the way, "...which the Father has"—what?— "fixed by His own authority." There's that sovereign election again. It's sovereign. They knew that. "Lord, is it at this time you are restoring the kingdom?" They knew that it was a divine work to do it. This is a perfect opportunity for Jesus to straighten things out. Dig a little into the text, verse 7, "which the Father has fixed." *Tithemi*: set, appointed. I love this. "Fixed" is in the aorist middle—"fixed for Himself." Fixed for Himself. It's about His glory. Right? It's about His exaltation. It's about the whole world finally seeing paradise regained. It's about God finally being glorified, who is so dishonored throughout human history. It's about the glory of God and the honor of Jesus Christ. And God the Father has fixed for Himself that time by His own authority. It is singular, unilateral. There is no other way to understand it. There's no replacement theology in the theology of Jesus! There's no supercessionism. This is a movement to establish that there is no earthly kingdom for Israel. That is absolutely foreign to the Old Testament and completely foreign to the New Testament. Jesus didn't say, "Where'd you get that crazy idea? Haven't you been listening?" They just couldn't know the season, the time. The Cross was always the plan. He said, you remember, in the eighteenth chapter of Luke, also recorded in Matthew and Mark, He said "We're going to Jerusalem. And you know what's going to happen?" If you put those three accounts together, "I'm going to be betrayed, I'm going to be handed over to the chief priests and the scribes, they're going to condemn me, they're going to hand me over to the Gentiles because they can't execute me." All this is in exact order. "Then when I'm handed over to the Gentiles, I'm going to be mocked, mistreated, spit on, scourged, crucified, and I'm rising again." That's not Plan B. In fact, if you think that's Plan B, you're a fool! And Jesus called you one, "Oh fools and slow of heart to believe all that the prophets have said," Luke 24.

So wherever this Amill thing came from, it didn't come from the Old Testament, it didn't come from New Testament Jews, and it didn't come from Jesus. You say, "Well, were the apostles Amill? How about Peter— was Peter Amill?" Acts 3. Maybe Peter was the first Amill guy. I love this. Acts 3:1,. Peter's preaching away,"Men of Israel,"and so forth. Verse 13, "The God of Abraham, Isaac, and Jacob, the God of our fathers, has glorified His servant Jesus, the one whom you delivered up"--there's that primary and secondary element-- "...and disowned in the presence of Pilate, whom he decided to release to you, you disowned the Holy and Righteous One and asked for a murderer to be granted to you, but put to death the Prince of life." Oh my, what an indictment! It couldn't be any worse, couldn't be any more horrific! Look what you've done! Verse 18, "But the things which God announced beforehand by the mouth of all the prophets, that His Christ should suffer, He's thus fulfilled." That's literal, isn't it?! That's literal, isn't it?! "Repent therefore and return, that your sins may be wiped away in order that times of refreshing may come from the presence of the Lord." The "times of refreshing" is a kingdom phrase. "...that He may send Jesus, the Christ appointed for you"--set for you, fixed for you—"whom heaven must receive until the period of restoration"—another kingdom term—"of all things about which God spoke by the mouth of His holy prophets from ancient time." And then I especially love verse 25, "And it is you who are the sons of the prophets and of the covenant which God made with your fathers." Does Peter cancel the covenant? What does he say? "You are the sons of the covenant which God made with your fathers, saying to Abraham, 'In your seed shall all the families of the earth be blessed,' For you first, God raised up His servant, Christ, sent Him to bless you by turning every one of you from your wicked ways." And He will do that; you're still the sons of the covenant. Perfect opportunity to cancel those promises.

How about James, the head of the Jerusalem church? Was he amillennial in his view? In the fifteenth chapter of Acts and verse 13, James answered, "Brethren, listen to me. Simeon has related how God first concerned Himself about taking from among the Gentiles a people for His name. And with this the words of the Prophets agree, just as it is written: 'After these things I will return, I will rebuild the tabernacle of David which has fallen, and I will rebuild its ruins, and I will restore it, in order that the rest of mankind may seek the Lord, and all the Gentiles who are called by My name,' says the Lord, 'Who make these things known from of old.'" The acceptance of the Gentiles is not the cancellation of promises to Israel. After Gentile conversion, after the times of the Gentiles are over, "I will rebuild the tabernacle of David which has fallen, ...rebuild its ruins, and...restore it." Davidic covenant promises, Messianic promises will be fulfilled.

Maybe the writer of Hebrews was an Amill. Chapter 6, verse 1,: "...when God made the promise to Abraham, since He could swear by no greater, He swore by Himself, saying 'I will surely bless you, I will surely multiply you.'" "I will. I will." No hesitation. No hesitation. And He calls on our understanding of swearing. "...men swear by one greater than themselves, with them an oath given as confirmation is an end of every dispute. In the same way God, desiring more to show to the heirs of the promise the unchangeableness of His purpose, interposed with an oath." God swears, makes an oath! And it's "...impossible," the next verse says, "for God to lie."

Maybe the apostle Paul was the first Amillennialist. Look at Romans 3, verse 1, "...what advantage has the Jew? Or what benefit of circumcision? Great in every respect. First of all...they were entrusted with the oracles of God. What then? If some did not believe, their unbelief will not nullify the faithfulness of God, will it?! May it never be!" And this is where Paul should have said, "Absolutely! Absolutely it nullifies the promise of God! Unquestionably it nullifies the promise of God!" Doesn't say that. Chapter 9, and verse 6, "...it is not as though the word of God has failed. For they are not all Israel who are descended from Israel." That is to say, they are not all true Israel, that is, believers. "...neither are they all children because they are Abraham's descendant, but: 'Through Isaac your descendants will be named.' That is, it is not the children of the flesh who are children of God, but the children of promise as regarded as descendants." There are children God has elected to fulfill His promise in. And He goes on to describe it, saying something as blatant as this, "Jacob I loved"-- verse 13--"Esau I hated." Verse 1, "I'll have mercy on whom I'll have mercy, I'll have compassion on whom I have compassion." Verse 16, "....it doesn't depend on the man who wills or the man who runs, but on God who has mercy." Verse 1, "He has mercy on whom He desires, He hardens whom He desires." This is back to this whole idea of sovereignty again! Just because there are some Jews that don't believe, does not nullify the faithfulness of God. Just because there are some that God chooses, doesn't mean that He's not going to choose a whole, duly-constituted generation of Jews to fulfill His promises.

And then, perhaps most notably (and we're hurrying a little bit) Romans 11. And I don't need to go into this— you know it very, very well. Romans 11:26, "...all Israel will be saved." How can you interpret that? One way! You tell me that's not Israel?! Where in the text does it say it's not Israel? I would understand if it said, "And God has cancelled His promises to Israel." But it says all Israel will be saved just as it is written "The Deliverer will come from Zion, will remove ungodliness from Jacob. This is My covenant with them when I take away their sins." Yes, they are enemies at the present time, but that is for the sake of the Gentiles. Verse 29, "...the gifts and the calling of God are irrevocable." And now we're back to where we started, right? Look, if it depended on them to obey on their own, was it was impossible from the start. Only the one who made the promise can enable the obedience that is connected to the fulfillment of the promise.

Now much more could be said about Romans 11. So when Jonathan Edwards wrote this: "Promises that were made by the prophets to the people of Israel concerning their future prosperity and glory are fulfilled in the Christian Church according to their proper intent." I say, where did he get that? Where did that come from? Didn't come from any passage that I can find. Let me just conclude with some effects and there is a lot more I could say. That's what we always say when we've just run out of material. You've really endured lengthy--but just a couple more comments.

I suggest for your reading *Israel and the Church* by Ronald Diprose. We should have some in the bookstore. It first appeared in Italian. It was a Ph.D. dissertation. It has no connection to traditional Dispensationalism. It's a really, really fine work on replacement theology. It shows the effect of this idea as forming the Church of the Dark Ages, explaining how the Church went from the New Testament concept of the Church to the sacerdotal, sacramental institutional system of the Dark Ages that we know as Roman Catholicism. Diprose lays much of that at the feet of replacement theology that rises out of Augustine and the few before him, Origen and Justin. Where did the Church ever come up with altars? There is no altar in the New Testament. Where did the Church ever come up with sacrifices? Where did the Church ever come up with a parallel sign to circumcision? Where did the Church ever come up with the priesthood? Where did the Church ever come up with ceremony and ritual and symbolism? Where did the Church ever come up with the idea that you should reintroduce mystery by speaking in a language that the people there couldn't understand? He replaced preaching with ritual. From the formation of the Church in those early centuries to the system of Roman Catholicism, all the trappings fit Old Testament Judaism. And the hierarchical, institutional, non-personal, non-organic, sacerdotal approach to the Church he traces largely to the influence of causing the Church to be the new Israel. Replacement theology justifies bringing in all the trappings of Judaism.

Another effect of replacement theology is the damage that it does to Jewish evangelism. Here's a little scenario: You are talking to a Jew. You say, "Jesus is the Messiah." "Really, where is the kingdom?" "Oh, it's here!" "Oh, it is? Well, why are we being killed all the time? Why are we being persecuted and why don't we have the land that was promised to us? And why don't we--why isn't the Messiah reigning in Jerusalem, and why isn't the peace and joy and gladness dominating the world, and why isn't the desert blooming and...?" "Oh, no, you don't understand. All that's not going to happen. You see, the problem is you're not God's people any more. We are." "Oh! I see, but this is the kingdom, and Jews are being killed and hated, and Jerusalem is under siege. This is the kingdom? If this is the kingdom, Jesus is not the Messiah. Can't be. It's ludicrous." No matter how many wonderful Jewish-Christian relationships we try to have with rabbis, this is a huge bone in the throat. Why can't Jesus be the Messiah? Because this isn't the kingdom. Unless you can say to a Jew "God will keep every single promise He made to you, and Jesus will fulfill every single promise, and that is why there are still Jews in the world, and that is why you are in the land and God is preparing for a great day of salvation in Israel; and Jesus is your Messiah. But look at Psalm 22 and Isaiah 53 and Zechariah 12:10 and understand that He had to come and die to ratify the New Covenant before He could forgive your sin, and the kingdom is coming. THAT you got a chance to communicate. The rest doesn't make sense. Now, if you get election right—divine, sovereign, gracious, unconditional, unilateral, irrevocable election--and then you get God right, and you get Israel right, and you get eschatology right, and guess what, men, then you can just open your Bible and preach your heart out of that text and say what it says. How freeing is that? You don't have to scramble around and find some bizarre interpretation. Get it right and God is glorified. Get it right and Christ is exalted. Get it right and the Holy Spirit is honored. Get it right and Scripture is clear. Get it right and the greatest historical illustration of God's work in the world is visible. Get it right and the meaning of mystery in the New Testament is maintained. Get it right and normal language is intact and Scripture wasn't written for mystics. Get it right and the chronology of prophetic literature is intact. Get it right and you shut out imagination from exegesis. Get it right and a historical worldview is complete. Get it right and the practical benefit of eschatology is released on your people. Get it right. The kingdom theology of the eschaton is the only view that honors sovereign, electing grace, honors the truthfulness of God's promises, honors the teaching of Old Testament prophets, the teaching of Jesus and the New Testament writers; that will allow Christ to be honored as supreme ruler over His creation now temporarily in the hands of Satan; and the earthly millennial kingdom established at Christ's return is the only and necessary bridge from temporary human history to eternal divine glory. Make your church a second coming church and make your life a second coming life. "

Again, quoting MacArthur:
"You say, well, didn't the Dispensationalists invent Premillennialism? Well, in the modern era two books really reintroduced Premillennial view--the biblical, the straightforward biblical view--neither of them written by a Dispensationalist. The first one was called The Premillennial Advent. It was written in 1815 by an Anglican named William Cunningham. The second one that reintroduced this into the more modern era was a publication in England in 1827 written by Emmanuel de Lacunza y Diaz, a Jesuit."

Further, history shows that Prior to Augustine, the Church Fathers taught pre-millenialism. Special thanks to Dr. Keith Sherlin for the following

2 Church Fathers on the Millennial Reign of Christ
Papias: AD 60 to 130; Student of Apostle John
"There will be a millennium after the resurrection of the dead, when the kingdom of Christ will be set up in material form on this earth." (Papias as quoted in Eusebius Ecclesiastical History, II vols, Cambridge, MA: Harvard University Press, 1926), Vol. I, p. 297).

Justin Martyr: AD 100 to 165
"But I and others, who are right-minded Christians on all points, are assured that there will be a resurrection of the dead, and a thousand years in Jerusalem, which will then be built, adorned, and enlarged, as the prophets Ezekiel and Isaiah and others declare." (Justin Martyr, Dialogue With Trypho, chapter 80.). Also he said, "And further, there was a certain man with us, whose name was John, one of the apostles of Christ, who prophesied, by a revelation that was made to him, that those who believed in our Christ would dwell a thousand years in Jerusalem; and that thereafter the general, and, in short, the eternal resurrection and judgment of all men would likewise take place" (Justin Martyr, Dialogue With Trypho, chapter 81).

A major bone of contention is Supersessionsism or Replacement Theology, if you like to call it that. Replacement Theology...

From gotquestions.org...
"Question: "What is replacement theology /supersessionism?"

Answer: Replacement theology (also known as supersessionism) essentially teaches that the church has replaced Israel in God's plan. Adherents of replacement theology believe the Jews are no longer God's chosen people, and God does not have specific future plans for the nation of Israel. All the different views of the relationship between the church and Israel can be divided into two camps: either the church is a continuation of Israel (replacement/covenant theology), or the church is completely different and distinct from Israel (dispensationalism/premillennialism).

Replacement theology teaches that the church is the replacement for Israel and that the many promises made to Israel in the Bible are fulfilled in the Christian church, not in Israel. So, the prophecies in Scripture concerning the blessing and restoration of Israel to the Promised Land are "spiritualized" or "allegorized" into promises of God's blessing for the church. Major problems exist with this view, such as the continuing existence of the Jewish people throughout the centuries and especially with the revival of the modern state of Israel. If Israel has been condemned by God, and there is no future for the Jewish nation, how do we explain the supernatural survival of the Jewish people over the past 2000 years despite the many attempts to destroy them? How do we explain why and how Israel reappeared as a nation in the 20th century after not existing for 1900 years?

The view that Israel and the church are different is clearly taught in the New Testament. Biblically speaking, the church is completely different and distinct from Israel, and the two are never to be confused or used interchangeably. We are taught from Scripture that the church is an entirely new creation that came into being on the day of Pentecost and will continue until it is taken to heaven at the rapture (Ephesians 1:9-11; 1 Thessalonians 4:13-17). The church has no relationship to the curses and blessings for Israel. The covenants, promises, and warnings are valid only for Israel. Israel has been temporarily set aside in God's program during these past 2000 years of dispersion.

After the rapture (1 Thessalonians 4:13-18), God will restore Israel as the primary focus of His plan. The first event at this time is the tribulation (Revelation chapters 6-19). The world will be judged for rejecting Christ, while Israel is prepared through the trials of the great tribulation for the second coming of the Messiah. Then, when Christ does return to the earth, at the end of the tribulation, Israel will be ready to receive Him. The remnant of Israel which survives the tribulation will be saved, and the Lord will establish His kingdom on this earth with Jerusalem as its capital. With Christ reigning as King, Israel will be the leading nation, and representatives from all nations will come to Jerusalem to honor and worship the King—Jesus Christ. The church will return with Christ and will reign with Him for a literal thousand years (Revelation 20:1-5).

Both the Old Testament and the New Testament support a premillennial/dispensational understanding of God's plan for Israel. Even so, the strongest support for premillennialism is found in the clear teaching of Revelation 20:1-7, where it says six times that Christ's kingdom will last 1000 years. After the tribulation the Lord will return and establish His kingdom with the nation of Israel, Christ will reign over the whole earth, and Israel will be the leader of the nations. The church will reign with Him for a literal thousand years. The church has not replaced Israel in God's plan. While God may be focusing His attention primarily on the church in this dispensation of grace, God has not forgotten Israel and will one day restore Israel to His intended role as the nation He has chosen (Romans 11). "

I would like to point out that there is not a single person alive who knows any Hittites. For that matter, you don't know any Amorites, Perrizites, Hivites, Jebusites, Amalekites or Canaanites either. I cannot tell you the last time I had coffee with an Agagite or lunch with a Philistine. That being the case, it must be significant that there is still an Israel but none of the others...

It is, precisely, the Amillenial viewpoint that causes me to reject Covenant Theology. Quoting Dr. MacArthur's lesson on how to interpret the Bible,

"There are no allegories in the Bible, it is normal language, it means exactly what it appears to mean. There is no deeper meaning, there's no hidden meaning, there's no secret meaning, there's no spiritualized meaning. Yes, they're prophetic passages where there are analogies, there are illustrations. You read Zechariah, Daniel, Ezekiel, Isaiah, in the book of Revelation you see images...those images are conveying a reality. They are conveying a reality in a symbolic way. And, you know, we use those kinds of things all the time, so did Jesus in parables, right? Parables were fictional stories conveying actual truth.

So you do not ever abandon literal interpretation in favor of some mystical, hidden allegorical interpretation which discards accuracy, coherence, intelligence and reason. Then you have a free-for-all...free-for-all. This also was the way the rabbis did it. The rabbis said Abraham had 318 servants because letters and...letters had a numerical equivalent and the consonants in Abraham's name added up to 318, so the fact that the consonants in Abraham's name added up to 318 meant that Abraham had 318 servants. That's just not true, that's irrelevant. It has nothing to do with the truth that's being conveyed with the name Abraham. But that kind of esoteric, quasi, Gnostic sort of elevated insight was very common among rabbis and we find a lot of it today in…it appears in numerology, sometimes you read about numbers in the Bible…sometimes you read about certain historical events appearing in the text of the bible if you go across the letters at an angle, or a diagonal or up or down or across and it gives all the events of history. You can throw those things in a computer. Somebody did that. Somebody said this is the secret meaning of the Bible, there are books that have been written on this. Somebody else put the same stuff together, threw it in a computer and accomplished exactly the same thing with Herman Melville's Moby Dick. And he wasn't divine, and he didn't write secret meanings in the letters on different rows and at different angles. So these kinds of things are crazy misguiding treatments of Scripture. So literal…literal."

Quoting John Calvin
This error [of allegory] has been the source of many evils. Not only did it open the way for the adulteration of the natural meaning of Scripture but also set up boldness in allegorizing as the chief exegetical virtue. Thus many of the ancients without any restraint played all sorts of games with the sacred Word of God, as if they were tossing a ball to and fro. It also gave heretics a chance to throw the Church into turmoil, for when it is accepted practice for anybody to interpret any passage in any way he desired, any mad idea, however absurd or monstrous, could be introduced under the pretext of allegory. Even good men were carried away by their mistaken fondness for allegories into formulating a great number of perverse opinions. (Commentary on 2 Corinthians 3:6)

Further, Calvin concluded that students of God's Word must "entirely reject the allegories of Origen, and of others like him, which Satan, with the deepest subtlety, has endeavored to introduce into the Church, for the purpose of rendering the doctrine of Scripture ambiguous and destitute of all certainty and firmness" (Commentary on Genesis 2:8).

If there are not allegories in the Bible, then it must, of necessity, mean that Amillenialism cannot be correct.

1925 Baptist Faith and Message Statement

I. The Scriptures

We believe that the Holy Bible was written by men divinely inspired, and is a perfect treasure of heavenly instruction; that it has God for its author, salvation for its end, and truth, without any mixture of error, for its matter; that it reveals the principles by which God will judge us; and therefore is, and will remain to the end of the world, the true center of Christian union, and the supreme standard by which all human conduct, creeds and religious opinions should be tried.

Luke 16:29-31; 2 Tim. 3:15-17; Eph. 2:20; Heb. 1:1; 2 Peter 1:19-21; John 16:13-15; Matt. 22:29-31; Psalm 19:7-10; Psalm 119:1-8.

II. God

There is one and only one living and true God, an intelligent, spiritual, and personal Being, the Creator, Preserver, and Ruler of the universe, infinite in holiness and all other perfections, to whom we owe the highest love, reverence, and obedience. He is revealed to us as Father, Son, and Holy Spirit, each with distinct personal attributes, but without division of nature, essence, or being.

Gen. 1:1; 1 Cor. 8:4-6; Deut. 6:4; Jer. 10:10; Isa. 48:12; Deut. 5:7; Ex. 3:14; Heb. 11:6; John 5:26; 1 Tim. 1:17; John 1:14-18; John 15:26; Gal. 4:6; Matt. 28:19.

III. The Fall of Man

Man was created by the special act of God, as recorded in Genesis. "So God created man in his own image, in the image of God created he him; male and female created he them" (Gen. 1:27). "And the Lord God formed man of the dust of the ground, and breathed into his nostrils the breath of life; and man became a living soul" (Gen. 2:7).

He was created in a state of holiness under the law of his Maker, but, through the temptation of Satan, he transgressed the command of God and fell from his original holiness and righteousness; whereby his posterity inherit a nature corrupt and in bondage to sin, are under condemnation, and as soon as they are capable of moral action, become actual transgressors.

Gen. 1:27; Gen. 2:7; John 1:23; Gen. 3:4-7; Gen. 3:22-24; Rom. 5:12,14,19, 21; Rom. 7:23-25; Rom. 11:18,22,32-33; Col. 1:21.

IV. The Way of Salvation

The salvation of sinners is wholly of grace, through the mediatorial office of the Son of God, who by the Holy Spirit was born of the Virgin Mary and took upon him our nature, yet without sin; honored the divine law by his personal obedience and made atonement for our sins by his death. Being risen from the dead, he is now enthroned in Heaven, and, uniting in his person the tenderest sympathies with divine perfections, he is in every way qualified to be a compassionate and all-sufficient Saviour.

Col. 1:21-22; Eph. 1:7-10; Gal. 2:19-20; Gal. 3:13; Rom. 1:4; Eph. 1:20-23; Matt. 1:21-25; Luke 1:35; 2:11; Rom. 3:25.

V. Justification

Justification is God's gracious and full acquittal upon principles of righteousness of all sinners who believe in Christ. This blessing is bestowed, not in consideration of any works of righteousness which we have done, but through the redemption that is in and through Jesus Christ. It brings us into a state of most blessed peace and favor with God, and secures every other needed blessing.

Rom. 3:24; 4:2; 5:1-2; 8:30; Eph. 1:7; 1 Cor. 1:30-31; 2 Cor. 5:21.

VI. The Freeness of Salvation

The blessings of salvation are made free to all by the gospel. It is the duty of all to accept them by penitent and obedient faith. Nothing prevents the salvation of the greatest sinner except his own voluntary refusal to accept Jesus Christ as teacher, Saviour, and Lord.

Eph. 1:5; 2:4-10; 1 Cor. 1:30-31; Rom. 5:1-9; Rev. 22:17; John 3:16; Mark 16:16.

VII. Regeneration

Regeneration or the new birth is a change of heart wrought by the Holy Spirit, whereby we become partakers of the divine nature and a holy disposition is given, leading to the love and practice of righteousness. It is a work of God's free grace conditioned upon faith in Christ and made manifest by the fruit which we bring forth to the glory of God.

John 3:1-8, 1:16-18; Rom. 8:2; Eph. 2:1,5-6,8,10; Eph. 4:30,32; Col. 3:1-11; Titus 3:5.

VIII. Repentance and Faith

We believe that repentance and faith are sacred duties, and also inseparable graces, wrought in our souls by the regenerating Spirit of God; whereby being deeply convinced of our guilt, danger, and helplessness, and of the way of

salvation by Christ, we turn to God with unfeigned contrition, confession, and supplication for mercy; at the same time heartily receiving the Lord Jesus Christ as our Prophet, Priest, and King, and relying on him alone as the only and all-sufficient Saviour.
Luke 22:31-34; Mark 1:15; 1 Tim. 1:13; Rom. 3:25,27,31; Rom. 4:3,9,12,16-17; John 16:8-11.

IX. God's Purpose of Grace
Election is the gracious purpose of God, according to which he regenerates, sanctifies and saves sinners. It is perfectly consistent with the free agency of man, and comprehends all the means in connection with the end. It is a most glorious display of God's sovereign goodness, and is infinitely wise, holy, and unchangeable. It excludes boasting and promotes humility. It encourages the use of means in the highest degree.
Rom. 8:30; 11:7; Eph. 1:10; Acts 26:18; Eph. 1:17-19; 2 Tim. 1:9; Psalm 110:3; 1 Cor. 2:14; Eph. 2:5; John 6:44-45,65; Rom. 10:12-15.

X. Sanctification
Sanctification is the process by which the regenerate gradually attain to moral and spiritual perfection through the presence and power of the Holy Spirit dwelling in their hearts. It continues throughout the earthly life, and is accomplished by the use of all the ordinary means of grace, and particularly by the Word of God.
Acts 20:32; John 17:17; Rom. 6:5-6; Eph. 3:16; Rom. 4:14; Gal. 5:24; Heb. 12:14; Rom. 7:18-25; 2 Cor. 3:18; Gal. 5:16,25-26.

XI. Perseverance
All real believers endure to the end. Their continuance in well-doing is the mark which distinguishes them from mere professors. A special Providence cares for them, and they are kept by the power of God through faith unto salvation.
John 10:28-29; 2 Tim. 2:19; 1 John 2:19; 1 Cor. 11:32; Rom. 8:30; 9:11,16; Rom. 5:9-10; Matt. 26:70-75.

XII. The Gospel Church
A church of Christ is a congregation of baptized believers, associated by covenant in the faith and fellowship of the gospel; observing the ordinances of Christ, governed by his laws, and exercising the gifts, rights, and privileges invested in them by his word, and seeking to extend the gospel to the ends of the earth. Its Scriptural officers are bishops, or elders, and deacons.
Matt. 16:18; Matt. 18:15-18; Rom. 1:7; 1 Cor. 1:2; Acts 2:41-42; 5:13-14; 2 Cor. 9:13; Phil. 1:1; 1 Tim. 4:14; Acts 14:23; Acts 6:3,5-6; Heb. 13:17; 1 Cor. 9:6,14.

XIII. Baptism and the Lord's Supper

Christian baptism is the immersion of a believer in water in the name of the Father, the Son, and the Holy Spirit. The act is a symbol of our faith in a crucified, buried and risen Saviour. It is prerequisite to the privileges of a church relation and to the Lord's Supper, in which the members of the church, by the use of bread and wine, commemorate the dying love of Christ.
Matt. 28:19-20; 1 Cor. 4:1; Rom. 6:3-5; Col. 2:12; Mark 1:4; Matt. 3:16; John 3:23; 1 Cor. 11:23-26; 1 Cor. 10:16-17,21; Matt. 26:26-27; Acts 8:38-39; Mark 1:9-11.

XIV. The Lord's Day

The first day of the week is the Lord's day. It is a Christian institution for regular observance. It commemorates the resurrection of Christ from the dead and should be employed in exercises of worship and spiritual devotion, both public and private, and by refraining from worldly amusements, and resting from secular employments, works of necessity and mercy only excepted.
Ex. 20:3-6; Matt. 4:10; Matt. 28:19; 1 Tim. 4:13; Col. 3:16; John 4:21; Ex. 20:8; 1 Cor. 16:1-2; Acts 20:7; Rev. 1:1; Matt. 12:1-13.

XV. The Righteous and the Wicked

There is a radical and essential difference between the righteous and wicked. Those only who are justified through the name of the Lord Jesus Christ and sanctified by the Holy Spirit are truly righteous in his sight. Those who continue in impenitence and unbelief are in his sight wicked and are under condemnation. This distinction between the righteous and the wicked holds in and after death, and will be made manifest at the judgment when final and everlasting awards are made to all men.
Gen. 3:19; Acts 13:36; Luke 23:43; 2 Cor. 5:1,6,8; Phil. 1:23; 1 Cor. 15:51-52; 1 Thess. 4:17; Phil. 3:21; 1 Cor. 6:3; Matt. 25:32-46; Rom. 9:22-23; Mark 9:48; 1 Thess. 1:7-10; Rev. 22:20.

XVI. The Resurrection

The Scriptures clearly teach that Jesus rose from the dead. His grave was emptied of its contents. He appeared to the disciples after his resurrection in many convincing manifestations. He now exists in his glorified body at God's right hand. There will be a resurrection of the righteous and the wicked. The bodies of the righteous will conform to the glorious spiritual body of Jesus.
1 Cor. 15:1-58; 2 Cor. 5:1-8; 1 Thess. 4:17; John 5:28-29; Phil. 3:21; Acts 24:15; John 20:9; Matt. 28:6.

XVII. The Return of the Lord

The New Testament teaches in many places the visible and personal return of Jesus to this earth. "This same Jesus which is taken up from you into heaven, shall so come in like manner as ye have seen him go into heaven." The time of

his coming is not revealed. "Of that day and hour knoweth no one, no, not the angels in heaven, but my Father only" (Matt. 24:36). It is the duty of all believers to live in readiness for his coming and by diligence in good works to make manifest to all men the reality and power of their hope in Christ.
Matt. 24:36; Matt. 24:42-47; Mark 13:32-37; Luke 21:27-28; Acts 1:9-11.

XVIII. Religious Liberty
God alone is Lord of the conscience, and he has left it free from the doctrines and commandments of men which are contrary to his Word or not contained in it. Church and state should be separate. The state owes to the church protection and full freedom in the pursuit of its spiritual ends. In providing for such freedom no ecclesiastical group or denomination should be favored by the state more than others. Civil government being ordained of God, it is the duty of Christians to render loyal obedience thereto in all things not contrary to the revealed will of God. The church should not resort to the civil power to carry on its work. The gospel of Christ contemplates spiritual means alone for the pursuit of its ends. The state has no right to impose penalties for religious opinions of any kind. The state has no right to impose taxes for the support of any form of religion. A free church in a free state is the Christian ideal, and this implies the right of free and unhindered access to God on the part of all men, and the right to form and propagate opinions in the sphere of religion without interference by the civil power.
Rom. 13:1-7; 1 Peter 2:17; 1 Tim. 2:1-2; Gal. 3:9-14; John 7:38-39; James 4:12; Gal. 5:13; 2 Peter 2:18-21; 1 Cor. 3:5; Rom. 6:1-2; Matt. 22:21; Mark 12:17.

XIX. Peace and War
It is the duty of Christians to seek peace with all men on principles of righteousness. In accordance with the spirit and teachings of Christ they should do all in their power to put an end to war.
The true remedy for the war spirit is the pure gospel of our Lord. The supreme need of the world is the acceptance of his teachings in all the affairs of men and nations, and the practical application of his law of love.
We urge Christian people throughout the world to pray for the reign of the Prince of Peace, and to oppose everything likely to provoke war.
Matt. 5:9,13-14,43-46; Heb. 12:14; James 4:1; Matt. 6:33; Rom. 14:17,19.

XX. Education
Christianity is the religion of enlightenment and intelligence. In Jesus Christ are hidden all the treasures of wisdom and knowledge. All sound learning is therefore a part of our Christian heritage. The new birth opens all human faculties and creates a thirst for knowledge. An adequate system of schools is necessary to a complete spiritual program for Christ's people. The cause of

education in the Kingdom of Christ is coordinate with the causes of missions and general benevolence, and should receive along with these the liberal support of the churches.
Deut. 4:1,5,9,13-14; Deut. 6:1,7-10; Psalm 19:7-8; Prov. 8:1-7; Prov. 4:1-10; Matt. 28:20; Col. 2:3; Neh. 8:1-4.

XXI. Social Service
Every Christian is under obligation to seek to make the will of Christ regnant in his own life and in human society to oppose in the spirit of Christ every form of greed, selfishness, and vice; to provide for the orphaned, the aged, the helpless, and the sick; to seek to bring industry, government, and society as a whole under the sway of the principles of righteousness, truth and brotherly love; to promote these ends Christians should be ready to work with all men of good will in any good cause, always being careful to act in the spirit of love without compromising their loyalty to Christ and his truth. All means and methods used in social service for the amelioration of society and the establishment of righteousness among men must finally depend on the regeneration of the individual by the saving grace of God in Christ Jesus.
Luke 10:25-37; Ex. 22:10,14; Lev. 6:2; Deut. 20:10; Deut. 4:42; Deut. 15:2; 27:17; Psalm 101:5; Ezek. 18:6; Heb. 2:15; Zech. 8:16; Ex. 20:16; James 2:8; Rom. 12-14; Col. 3:12-17.

XXII. Co-Operation
Christ's people should, as occasion requires, organize such associations and conventions as may best secure co-operation for the great objects of the Kingdom of God. Such organizations have no authority over each other or over the churches. They are voluntary and advisory bodies designed to elicit, combine, and direct the energies of our people in the most effective manner. Individual members of New Testament churches should co-operate with each other, and the churches themselves should co-operate with each other in carrying forward the missionary, educational, and benevolent program for the extension of Christ's Kingdom. Christian unity in the New Testament sense is spiritual harmony and voluntary co-operation for common ends by various groups of Christ's people. It is permissable and desirable as between the various Christian denominations, when the end to be attained is itself justified, and when such co-operation involves no violation of conscience or compromise of loyalty to Christ and his Word as revealed in the New Testament.
Ezra 1:3-4; 2:68-69; 5:14-15; Neh. 4:4-6; 8:1-4; Mal. 3:10; Matt. 10:5-15; 20:1-16; 22:1-10; Acts 1:13-14; 1:21:26; 2:1,41-47; 1 Cor. 1:10-17; 12:11-12; 13; 14:33-34,40; 16:2; 2 Cor. 9:1-15; Eph. 4:1-16; 3 John 1:5-8.

XXIII. Evangelism and Missions

It is the duty of every Christian man and woman, and the duty of every church of Christ to seek to extend the gospel to the ends of the earth. The new birth of man's spirit by God's Holy Spirit means the birth of love for others.

Missionary effort on the part of all rests thus upon a spiritual necessity of the regenerate life. It is also expressly and repeatedly commanded in the teachings of Christ. It is the duty of every child of God to seek constantly to win the lost to Christ by personal effort and by all other methods sanctioned by the gospel of Christ.

Matt. 10:5; 13:18-23; 22:9-10; 28:19-20; Mark 16:15-16; 16:19-20; Luke 24:46-53; Acts 1:5-8; 2:1-2,21,39; 8:26-40; 10:42-48; 13:2,30-33; 1 Thess. 1-8.

XXIV. Stewardship

God is the source of all blessings, temporal and spiritual; all that we have and are we owe to him. We have a spiritual debtorship to the whole world, a holy trusteeship in the gospel, and a binding stewardship in our possessions. We are therefore under obligation to serve him with our time, talents and material possessions; and should recognize all these as entrusted to us to use for the glory of God and helping others. Christians should cheerfully, regularly, systematically, proportionately, and liberally, contribute of their means to advancing the Redeemer's cause on earth.

Luke 12:42; 16:1-8; Titus 1:7; 1 Peter 4:10; 2 Cor. 8:1-7; 2 Cor. 8:11-19; 2 Cor. 12:1-15; Matt. 25:14-30; Rom. 1:8-15; 1 Cor. 6:20; Acts 2:44-47.

XXV. The Kingdom

The Kingdom of God is the reign of God in the heart and life of the individual in every human relationship, and in every form and institution of organized human society. The chief means for promoting the Kingdom of God on earth are preaching the gospel of Christ, and teaching the principles of righteousness contained therein. The Kingdom of God will be complete when every thought and will of man shall be brought into captivity to the will of Christ. And it is the duty of all Christ's people to pray and labor continually that his Kingdom may come and his will be done on earth as it is done in heaven.

Dan. 2:37-44; 7:18; Matt. 4:23; 8:12; 12:25; 13:38,43; 25:34; 26:29; Mark 11:10; Luke 12:32; 22:29; Acts 1:6; 1 Cor. 15:24; Col. 1:13; Heb. 12:28; Rev. 1:9; Luke 4:43; 8:1; 9:2; 17:20-21; John 3:3; John 18:36; Matt. 6:10; Luke 23:42.

Part 2: Rightly Dividing the Word of Truth

As an added resource, I am including the premier work from C.I. Scofield, Rightly Dividing the Word of Truth. It is my sincere hope that this additional work will help you to further grow in grace and in knowledge for Christ's glory.

INTRODUCTION

In 2 Timothy 2 the believer is presented in seven characters. He is called a son (verse 1), a soldier (verse 3), an athlete (verse 5), a husbandman (verse 6), a workman (verse 15), a vessel (verse 21), and a servant (verse 24).

With each of these characters there is a well-suited exhortation. As a son, Timothy is exhorted to be strong in grace. Grace goes with sonship, just as law goes with servitude-as we learn from Galatians. Then, as a soldier, Timothy is exhorted to endure hardness and to avoid worldly entanglements; these are right elements of good soldiership. As a vessel, he is to be cleansed, separated; as a servant, gentle, patient, meek; and so of each of these seven aspects of his life as a Christian.

In 2 Timothy 15 he is told what is required of him as a workman: "Study to show thyself approved unto God, a workman that needeth not to be ashamed, rightly dividing the word of truth."

The Word of truth, then, has right divisions, and it must be evident that, as one cannot be "a workman that needeth not to be ashamed" without observing them, so any study of that Word which ignores those divisions must be in large measure profitless and confusing. Many Christians freely confess that they find the study of the Bible weary work. More find it so, who are ashamed to make the confession.

The purpose of this pamphlet is to indicate the more important divisions of the Word of truth. That this could not be fully done short of a complete analysis of the Bible is, of course, evident. But it is believed that enough is given to enable the diligent student to perceive the greater outlines of truth and something of the ordered beauty and symmetry of that Word of God which, to the natural mind, seems a mere confusion of inharmonious and conflicting ideas.

The student is earnestly exhorted not to receive a single doctrine upon the authority of this book, but, like the noble Bereans (Acts 17: 11), to search the Scriptures daily whether these things are so. No appeal is made to human authority. "The anointing which ye have received of him abideth in you, and ye need not that any man teach you" (I John 2:27).

Chapter 1
THE JEW, THE GENTILE, AND THE CHURCH OF GOD
Give none offence, neither to the Jews, nor to the Gentiles, nor to the church of God -- I Corinthians 10:32

Whoever reads the Bible with any attention cannot fail to perceive that more than half of its contents relate to one nation: the Israelites. He perceives, too, that they have a distinct place in the dealings and counsels of God. Separated from the mass of mankind, they are taken into covenant with Jehovah, who gives them specific promises not given to any other nation. Their history alone is told in Old Testament narrative and prophecy; other nations are mentioned only as they touch the Jew. It appears, also, that all the communications of Jehovah to Israel as a nation relate to the Earth. If faithful and obedient, the nation is promised earthly greatness, riches, and power; if unfaithful and disobedient, it is to be scattered 11 among all people, from the one end of the earth even unto the other" (Deut. 28:64). Even the promise of the Messiah is of blessing to "all the families of the Earth."

Continuing his research, the student finds mention in Scripture of another distinct body, which is called the church. This body also has a peculiar relation to God and, like Israel, has received from Him specific promises. But similarity ends there, and the most striking contrast begins. Instead of being formed of the natural descendants of Abraham alone, it is a body in which the distinction of Jew and Gentile is lost. Instead of the relation being one of mere covenant, it is one of birth. Instead of obedience bringing the reward of earthly greatness and wealth, the church is taught to be content with food and raiment, and to expect persecution and hatred; it is perceived that just as distinctly as Israel stands connected with temporal and earthly things, so distinctly does the church stand connected with spiritual and heavenly things.

Further, Scripture shows the student that neither Israel nor the church always existed; each had a recorded beginning. The beginning of Israel he finds in the call of Abram. Looking then for the birth of the church he finds (contrary, perhaps, to his expectations, for he has probably been taught that Adam and the patriarchs are in the church) that it certainly did not exist before, nor during, the earth life of Christ, for he finds Him speaking of His church as yet future when He says (Matt. 16:18), "Upon this rock I will build my church." Not, have built, nor am building, but will build.

He finds, too, from Ephesians 3:5-10, that the church is not once mentioned in Old Testament prophecy, but was, in those ages, a mystery "hid in God." Scripturally, he finds the birth of the church in Acts 2, and the termination of its career on the earth in I Thessalonians 4.

The student also finds, in the scriptural division of the race, another class, rarely mentioned, and distinguished in every respect from either Israel or the church: the Gentiles. The comparative position of the Jew, the Gentile, and the church may be briefly seen in the following Scriptures: the Jew (Rom. 9:4-5; John 4:22; Rom. 3:1-2); the Gentile (Eph. 2:11-12; Eph. 4:17-18; Mark 7:27-28); the Church (Eph. 1:22-23; Eph. 5:29-33; 1 Pet. 2:9).
Comparing, then, what is said in Scripture concerning Israel and the Church, he finds that in origin, calling, promise, worship, principles of conduct, and future destiny that all is contrast. Compare first the calling of Israel with that of the church.

ISRAEL
Now the LORD had said unto Abram, Get thee out of thy country, and from thy kindred, and from thy father's house unto a land that I will show thee (Gen. 12: 1).

For the LORD thy God bringeth thee into a good land, a land of brooks of water, of fountains and depths that spring out of valleys and hills; a land of wheat, and barley, and vines, and fig-trees, and pomegranates; a land of oil olive, and honey; a land wherein thou shalt eat bread without scarceness (Deut. 8:7-9).

And he said, I am Abraham's servant. And the LORD hath blessed my master greatly, and he is become great; and he hath given him flocks, and herds, and silver, and gold, and men-servants, and maid- servants, and camels, and asses (Gen. 24:34-35).

The LORD shall cause thine enemies that rise up against thee to be smitten before thy face: they shall come out against thee one way, and flee before thee seven ways (Deut. 28:7). And the LORD shall make thee the head, and not the tail; and thou shalt be above only, and thou shalt not be beneath (Deut. 28:13).

CHURCH
Wherefore, holy brethren, partakers of the heavenly calling (Heb. 3: 1).

For our conversation is in heaven (Phil. 3:20).

And Jesus saith unto him, The foxes have holes, and the birds of the air have nests; but the Son of man hath not where to lay his head (Matt. 8:20).

To an inheritance incorruptible, and undefiled, and that fadeth not away, reserved in heaven for you (I Pet. 1:4).

Even unto this present hour we both hunger, and thirst, and are naked, and are buffeted, and have no certain dwelling-place (I Cor. 4: 11).

And Jesus looked round about, and saith unto his disciples, How hardly shall they that have riches enter into the kingdom of God! (Mark 10:23).

Hearken, my beloved brethren, Hath not God chosen the poor of this world rich in faith, and heirs of the kingdom which he hath promised to them that love him? (James 2:5).

They shall put you out of the synagogues: yea, the time cometh that whosoever killeth you will think that he doeth God service (John 16:2).

Whosoever therefore shall humble himself as this little child, the same is greatest in the kingdom of heaven (Matt. 18:4).

Of course it is not meant that a godly Jew did not, at death, go to heaven. The distinction is that the incentive to godliness in his case was earthly blessings, not heavenly. It should be needless to say that, in this dispensation, neither Jew nor Gentile can be saved otherwise than by the exercise of that faith on the Lord Jesus Christ whereby both are born again (John 3:3, 16) and are baptized into that "one body" (I Con 12:13) which is "the church" (Eph. 1:22-23). In the church the distinction of Jew and Gentile disappears. (I Cor. 12:13; Gal. 3:28; Eph. 2:14. So in writing to the Ephesians the apostle speaks of them as "in time past Gentiles," Eph. 2:11; 1 Cor. 12:2, also says, "ye were Gentiles.")

The contrast between Israel and the church further appears in the rules given for the conduct of each.

ISRAEL

When the LORD thy God shall bring thee into the land whither thou goest to possess it, and hath cast out many nations before thee . . . thou shalt smite them, and utterly destroy them: thou shalt make no covenant with them, nor show mercy unto them (Deut. 7:1-2).

Eye for eye, tooth for tooth, hand for hand, foot for foot, burning for burning, wound for wound, stripe for stripe (Exod. 21:24-25).

CHURCH

But I say unto you, Love your enemies, bless them that curse you, do good to them that hate you, and pray for them which despitefully use you, and persecute you (Matt. 5:44).

Being reviled, we bless; being persecuted, we suffer it: being defamed, we entreat (I Cor. 4:12-13).

But I say unto you, That ye resist not evil: but whosoever shall smite thee on thy right cheek, turn to him the other also (Matt. 5:39).

See also: Deuteronomy 21:18-21 and Luke 15:20-23.

In the appointments for worship we still find contrast. Israel could worship in but one place and at a distance from God-only approaching Him through a priest. The church worships wherever two or three are gathered, has boldness to enter into the holiest, and is composed of priests. Compare Leviticus 17:8- 9 with Matthew 18:20, Luke 1:10 with Hebrews 10:19-20, Numbers 3:10 with I Peter 2:5.

In the predictions concerning the future of Israel and the church, the distinction is still more startling. The church will be taken away from the earth entirely, but restored Israel is yet to have her greatest earthly splendor and power. See what Scripture says as to

ISRAEL

"And, behold, thou shalt conceive in thy womb, and bring forth a son, and shalt call his name Jesus. He shall be great, and shall be called the Son of the Highest: and the Lord God shall give unto him the throne of his father David: and he shall reign over the house of Jacob forever; and of his kingdom there shall be no end" (Luke 1:31-33). (Of these seven promises to Maryfive have already been literally fulfilled. By what rule of interpretation are we authorized to say the remaining two will not be also fulfilled?)

"Simeon hath declared how God at the first did visit the Gentiles, to take out of them a people for his name. And to this agree the words of the prophets, as it is written: After this I will return, and will build again the tabernacle of David, which is fallen down; and I will build again the ruins thereof, and I will set it up" (Acts 15; 14-16).

"I say then, Hath God cast away his people? God forbid. For I also am an Israelite, of the seed of Abraham, of the tribe of Benjamin. I say then, Have they stumbled that they should fall? God forbid: but rather through their fall salvation is come unto the Gentiles, for to provoke them to jealousy. For if thou wert cut out of the olive tree which is wild by nature, and wert graffed contrary to nature into a good olive tree; how much more shall these, which be the natural branches, be graffed into their own olive tree? For I would not, brethren, that ye should be ignorant of this mystery, lest ye should be wise in your own conceits; that blindness in part is happened to Israel, until the fulness of the Gentiles be come in. And so all Israel shall be saved: as it is written, There shall come out of Sion the Deliverer, and shall turn away ungodliness from Jacob" (Rom. 11:1,11, 24-26).

"And it shall come to pass in that day, that the Lord shall set his hand again the second time to recover the remnant of his people.... And he shall set up an ensign for the nations, and shall assemble the outcasts of Israel, and gather together the dispersed of Judah from the four corners of the earth" (Isa. It: It - 12).

"For the Lord will have mercy on Jacob and will yet choose Israel, and set them in their own land: and the strangers shall be joined with them, and they shall cleave to the house of Jacob" (Isa. 14:1).

"Therefore, behold, the days come, saith the Lord, that it shall no more be said, The Lord liveth that brought up the children of Israel out of the land of Egypt; but, The Lord liveth that brought up the children of Israel from the land of the north, and from all the lands whither he had driven them: and I will bring them again into the land that I gave unto their fathers" (Jer. 16:14-15). "Behold, the days come, saith the Lord, that I will raise unto David a righteous Branch, and a King shall reign and prosper, and shall execute judgment and justice in the earth. In his days Judah shall be saved, and Israel shall dwell safely; and this is his name whereby he shall be called, THE LORD OUR RIGHTEOUSNESS" (Jer. 23:5-6).

"Behold, I will gather them out of all countries whither I have driven them in mine anger, and in my fury, and in great wrath; and I will bring them again unto this place, and I will cause them to dwell safely: and they shall be my people, and I will be their God" (Jer. 32:37,38).

"Sing, O daughter of Zion; shout, O Israel; be glad and rejoice with all the heart, 0 daughter of Jerusalem. The LORD hath taken away thy judgments, he hath cast out thine enemy: the King of Israel, even the LORD, is in the midst of thee: thou shalt not see evil any more" (Zeph. 3:14-15).

THE CHURCH

In my Father's house are many mansions: if it were not so, I would have told you. I go to prepare a place for you. And if I go and prepare a place for you, I will come again, and receive you unto myself; that where I am, there ye may be also" (John 14:2, 3).

"For this we say unto you by the word of the Lord, that we which are alive, and remain unto the coming of the Lord, shall not prevent [precede] them which are asleep. For the Lord himself shall descend from heaven with a shout, with the voice of the archangel, and with the trump of God: and the dead in Christ shall rise first: then we which are alive and remain shall be caught up together with them in the clouds to meet the Lord in the air: and so shall we ever be with the Lord (I Thess. 4:15-17).

"For our conversation is in heaven; from whence also we look for the Saviour, the Lord Jesus Christ: Who shall change our vile body, that it may be fashioned like unto his glorious body, according to the working whereby he is able even to subdue all things unto himself." (Phil. 3:20, 21).

"Beloved, now are we the sons of God; and it doth not yet appear what we shall be: but we know that, when he shall appear, we shall be like him; for we shall see him as he is" (I John 3:2).

"Let us be glad and rejoice, and give honor to him: for the marriage of the Lamb is come, and his wife hath made herself ready. And to her was granted that she should be arrayed in fine linen, clean and white: for the fine linen is the righteousness of saints. And he saith unto me, Write, Blessed are they which are called unto the marriage supper of the Lamb" (Rev. 19:7-9).

"Blessed and holy is he that hath part in the first resurrection: on such the second death hath no power, but they shall be priests of God and of Christ, and shall reign with him a thousand years" (Rev. 20:6).

It may safely be said that the Judaizing of the church has done more to hinder her progress, pervert her mission, and destroy her spiritually than all other causes combined. Instead of pursuing her appointed path of separation from the world and following the Lord in her heavenly calling, she has used Jewish Scriptures to justify herself in lowering her purpose to the civilization of the world, the acquisition of wealth, the use of an imposing ritual, the erection of magnificent churches, the invocation of God's blessing upon the conflicts of armies, and the division of an equal brotherhood into "clergy" and "laity."

Chapter 2
THE SEVEN DISPENSATIONS

The Scriptures divide time (by which is meant the entire period from the creation of Adam to the "new heaven and a new earth" of Rev. 21: 1) into seven unequal periods, usually called dispensations (Eph. 3:2), although these periods are also called ages (Eph. 2:7) and days, as in "day of the Lord."

These periods are marked off in Scripture by some change in God's method of dealing with mankind, or a portion of mankind, in respect of the two questions: of sin, and of man's responsibility. Each of the dispensations may be regarded as a new test of the natural man, and each ends in judgment, marking his utter failure in every dispensation. Five of these dispensations, or periods of time, have been fulfilled; we are living in the sixth, probably toward its close, and have before us the seventh, and last: the millennium.

1. **Man innocent**. This dispensation extends from the creation of Adam in Genesis 2:7 to the expulsion from Eden. Adam, created innocent and ignorant of good and evil, was placed in the garden of Eden with his wife, Eve, and put under responsibility to abstain from the fruit of the tree of the knowledge of good and evil. The dispensation of innocence resulted in the first failure of man, and in its far-reaching effects, the most disastrous. It closed in judgment: "So he drove out the man." See Gen. 1:26; Gen. 2:16,17; Gen. 3:6; Gen. 3:22-24.)

2. **Man under conscience**. By the fall, Adam and Eve acquired and transmitted to the race the knowledge of good and evil. This gave conscience a basis for right moral judgment, and hence the race came under this measure of responsibility-to do good and eschew evil. The result of the dispensation of conscience, from Eden to the flood (while there was no institution of government and of law), was that "all flesh had corrupted his way on the earth," that "the wickedness of man was great in the earth, and that every imagination of the thoughts of his heart was only evil continually," and God closed the second testing of the natural man with judgment: the flood. See Gen. 3:7, 22; Gen. 6:5,11-12; Gen. 7:11-12, 23.)

3. **Man in authority over the earth**. Out of the fearful judgment of the flood God saved eight persons, to whom, after the waters were assuaged, He gave the purified earth with ample power to govern it. This, Noah and his descendants were responsible to do. The dispensation of human government resulted, upon the plain of Shinar, in the impious attempt to become independent of God and closed in judgment: the confusion of tongues. (See

Gen. 9: 1, 2; Gen. 11: 1-4; Gen. 11:5-8.)

4. **Man under promise**. Out of the dispersed descendants of the builders of Babel, God called one man, Abram, with whom He enters into covenant. Some of the promises to Abram and his descendants were purely gracious and unconditional. These either have been or will yet be literally fulfilled. Other promises were conditional upon the faithfulness and obedience of the Israelites. Every one of these conditions was violated, and the dispensation of promise resulted in the failure of Israel and closed in the judgment of bondage in Egypt.

The book of Genesis, which opens with the sublime words, "In the beginning God created," closes with, "In a coffin in Egypt." (See Gen. 12:1-3; Gen. 13:14-17; Gen. 15:5; Gen. 26:3; Gen. 28:12-13; Exod. 1: 13-14.)

5. **Man under law**. Again the grace of God came to the help of helpless man and redeemed the chosen people out of the hand of the oppressor. In the wilderness of Sinai He proposed to them the covenant of law. Instead of humbly pleading for a continued relation of grace, they presumptuously answered: "All that the Lord hath spoken we will do." The history of Israel in the wilderness and in the land is one long record of flagrant, persistent violation of the law, and at last, after multiplied warnings, God closed the testing of man by law in judgment: first Israel, and then Judah, were driven out of the land into a dispersion which still continues. A feeble remnant returned under Ezra and Nehemiah, of which, in due time, Christ came: "Born of a woman-made under the law." Both Jews and Gentiles conspired to crucify Him. (See Exod. 19:1-8; 2 Kings 17:1-18; 2 Kings 25: 1 -11; Acts 2:22-23; Acts 7:5152; Rom. 3:19-20; Rom. 10:5; Gal. 3: 10.)

6. **Man under grace**. The sacrificial death of the Lord Jesus Christ introduced the dispensation of pure grace, which means undeserved favor, or God giving righteousness, instead of God requiring righteousness, as under law. Salvation, perfect and eternal, is now freely offered to Jew and Gentile upon the acknowledgment of sin, or repentance, with faith in Christ.

"Jesus answered and said unto them, This is the work of God, that ye believe on him whom he hath sent" (John 6:29). "Verily, verily, I say unto you, He that believeth on me hath everlasting life" (John 6:47). "Verily, verily, I say unto you, He that heareth my word, and believeth on him that sent me, hath everlasting life, and shall not come into condemnation; but is passed from death unto life." (John 5:24). "My sheep hear my voice, and I know them, and they follow me: and I give unto them eternal life; and they shall never perish" (John 10:27-28). "For by grace are ye saved through faith; and that not of yourselves: it is the gift of God: Not of works, lest any man should boast"

(Eph. 2:8-9).

The predicted result of this testing of man under grace is judgment upon an unbelieving world and an apostate church. (See Luke 17:26-30; Luke 18:8; 2 Thess. 2:7-12; Rev. 3:15-16.)

The first event in the closing of this dispensation will be the descent of the Lord from heaven, when sleeping saints will be raised and, together with believers then living, caught up "to meet the Lord in the air: and so shall we ever be with the Lord" (I Thess. 4:16-17). Then follows the brief period called "the great tribulation." (See Jer. 30:5-7; Dan. 12:1; Zeph. 1:15-18; Matt. 24:21-22.)

After this the personal return of the Lord to the earth in power and great glory occurs, and the judgments which introduce the seventh, and last dispensation. (See Matt. 25:31-46 and Matt. 24:29- 30.)

7. **Man under the personal reign of Christ**. After the purifying judgments which attend the personal return of Christ to the earth, He will reign over restored Israel and over the earth for one thousand years. This is the period commonly called the millennium. The seat of His power will be Jerusalem, and the saints, including the saved of the dispensation of grace, namely the church, will be associated with Him in His glory. (See Isa. 2:1-4; Isa. 11; Acts 15:14-17; Rev. 19:11-21; Rev. 20:1-6.

But when Satan is "loosed a little season," he finds the natural heart as prone to evil as ever, and easily gathers the nations to battle against the Lord and His saints, and this last dispensation closes, like all the others, in judgment. The great white throne is set, the wicked dead are raised and finally judged, and then come the "new heaven and a new earth." Eternity is begun. (See Rev. 20:3,7-15; Rev. 21 and 22.)

Chapter 3
THE TWO ADVENTS
When it testified beforehand the sufferings of Christ, and the glory that should follow I Peter 1: 11

Whoever carefully considers Old Testament prophecies must be struck by two contrasting and seemingly contradictory lines of prediction concerning the coming Messiah. One body of prediction speaks of Him as coming in weakness and humiliation, a man of sorrows and acquainted with grief, as a root out of dry ground, having no form nor comeliness, nor beauty that He should be desired. His visage is to be marred, His hands and feet pierced, He is to be forsaken of man and of God, and to make His grave with the wicked. (See Ps. 22:1-18; Isa. 7:14; Isa. 53; Dan. 9:26; Zech. 13:6-7; Mark 14:27.)

The other line of prophecy foretells a splendid and resistless Sovereign, purging the earth with awful judgments, regathering dispersed Israel, restoring the throne of David in more than Solomon's splendor, and introducing a reign of profound peace and perfect righteousness. (See Deut. 30:1-7; Isa. 11:1-2, 10-12; Isa. 9:6-7; Isa. 24:21-23; Isa. 40:9-11; Jer. 23:5-8; Dan. 7:13-14; Mic. 5:2; Matt. 1: 1; Matt. 2:2; Luke 1:31-33.)

In due time the fulfillment of messianic prophecy began with the birth of the virgin's Son according to Isaiah, in Bethlehem according to Micah, and proceeded with perfect literalness unto the full accomplishment of every prediction of Messiah's humiliation; for sin must first be put away, before the kingdom could be established. But the Jews would not receive their King in the form in which He was presented, "meek and sitting upon an ass and a colt the foal of an ass," and they crucified Him. (See Zech. 9:9 with Matt. 21:1-5; John 19:15-16.)

But we must not conclude that the wickedness of man has baffled the deliberate purpose of God, for His counsels include a second advent of His Son, when the predictions concerning Messiah's earthly glory will receive the same precise and literal fulfillment as did those which concerned His earthly sufferings. (See Hos. 3:4-5; Matt. 24:27-30; Luke 1:31-33; Acts 1:6-7; Acts 15:14-17.)

The Jews were slow of heart to believe all that the prophets had spoken concerning the sufferings of their Messiah; we are slow of heart to believe all that they have spoken concerning His glory. Surely the greater reproach is ours, for it ought to be easier to believe that the Son of God would come "in the clouds of heaven, with power and great glory" than that He would come as the babe of Bethlehem and the carpenter of Nazareth. Indeed, we believe the latter because it has happened, not because the prophets foretold it, and it is time we ceased to reproach the Jews for their unbelief. If it be asked how they could possibly be blinded to the evident meaning of so many and such unequivocal predictions, the answer is that they were blinded in exactly the same way that many Christians are blinded to the equally evident meaning of a far greater number of predictions of His earthly glory, namely, by the process of "spiritualizing" Scripture. In other words, the ancient scribes told the people that the prophecies of Messiah's sufferings were not to be interpreted literally, just as some modern scribes are telling the people that the prophecies of Messiah's earthly glory are not to be literally interpreted.

The second advent is a promise to the church as well as to the Jew. Among the last words of comfort and exhortation addressed by our Lord to His perplexed and sorrowing disciples before He accomplished the sacrifice of the cross were these: "Let not your heart be troubled: ye believe in God, believe also in me. In my Father's house are many mansions: if it were not so, I would have told you. I go to prepare a place for you. And if I go and prepare a place for you, I will come again, and receive you unto myself; that where I am, there ye may be also" (John 14:1-3).

Here the Lord speaks of His coming again in precisely the same terms as of His departure. The latter was, we know, personal and bodily. If we say that the former is impersonal and "spiritual," surely to such a forced interpretation of simple language we ought to be constrained only by the most imperative and unqualified Scripture elsewhere. But no such passages exist. But we are not left to doubt upon this vital point, nor to draw conclusions of reason, however irresistible.

In the very moment of our Lord's disappearance from the sight of His disciples, "Two men stood by them in white apparel; which also said, Ye men of Galilee, why stand ye gazing up into heaven? This same Jesus, which is taken up from you into heaven, shall so come in like manner as ye have seen him go into heaven" (Acts 1:10-11).

To the same purport is I Thess. 4:16-17: "For the Lord himself shall descend from heaven with a shout, with the voice of the archangel, and with the trump of God: and the dead in Christ shall rise first: then we which are alive and remain shall be caught up together with them in the clouds, to meet the Lord in the air; and so shall we ever be with the Lord." "Looking for that blessed hope, and the glorious appearing of the great God and our Saviour Jesus Christ" (Titus 2:13).

"For our citizenship is in heaven; from whence also we wait for a Saviour, the Lord Jesus Christ: who shall fashion anew the body of our humiliation, that it may be cFor our conversation is in heaven; from whence also we look for the Saviour, the Lord Jesus Christ: Who shall change our vile body, that it may be fashioned like unto his glorious body, according to the working whereby he is able even to subdue all things unto himself." (Phil. 3:20-21).

"Beloved, now are we the sons of God; and it doth not yet appear what we shall be: but we know that, when he shall appear, we shall be like him; for we shall see him as he is" (I John 3:2). "And behold, I come quickly; and my reward is with me, to give every man according as his work shall be" (Rev. 22:12).

For this "blessed hope" we are taught to "watch" (Mark 13:33, 35, 37; Matt. 24:42; 25:13), "wait" (I Thess. 1: 10), and be "ready" (Matt. 24:44). The last prayer in the Bible is one for Christ's speedy return (Rev. 22:20).

By these Scriptures it abundantly appears that the second advent will be personal and bodily. Therefore it does not mean the death of the believer, nor the destruction of Jerusalem, nor the descent of the Holy Spirit at Pentecost, nor the gradual diffusion of Christianity, but that it is the "blessed hope" of the church, the time when sleeping saints will be raised, and, together with saints then living, who will be "changed" (I Cor. 15:51-52), caught up to meet the Lord-the time when we who are now the sons of God will be like Him and when faithful saints will be rewarded for works of faith, for His name's sake, after they have been saved.

The following Scriptures will further bring into view the contrast between the two advents of our Lord. Compare the first advent with the second.

FIRST ADVENT

And she brought forth her first-born son, and wrapped him in swaddling clothes, and laid him in a manger; because there was no room for them in the inn (Luke 2:7).

But now once in the end of the world hath he appeared to put away sin by the sacrifice of himself (Heb. 9:26).

For the Son of man is come to seek and to save that which was lost (Luke 19:10).

For God sent not his Son into the world to condemn the world; but that the world through him might be saved (John 3:17).

And if any man hear my words, and believe not, I judge him not: for I came not to judge the world, but to save the world (John 12:47).

SECOND ADVENT

And then shall appear the sign of the Son of man, in heaven: and then shall all the tribes of the earth mourn, and they shall see the Son of man coming in the clouds of heaven with power and great glory (Matt. 24:30).

So Christ was once offered to bear the sins of many; and unto them that look for him shall he appear the second time, without sin, unto salvation (Heb. 9:28).

And to you who are troubled, rest with us: when the Lord Jesus shall be revealed from heaven with his mighty angels, in flaming fire taking vengeance on them that know not God, and that obey not the gospel of our Lord Jesus Christ (2 Thess. 1:7-8).

Because he hath appointed a day, in the which he will judge the world in righteousness, by that man whom he hath ordained; whereof he hath given assurance unto all men, in that he hath raised him from the dead (Acts 17:31).

The student may multiply these contrasts almost indefinitely. Enough, however, has been put forth that both the promises to Israel and to the church imperatively require a return of our Lord to the earth.

It may be helpful to beginning Bible students to consider, briefly, the various theories which are put forward to oppose the scriptural doctrine of the personal and corporeal return, or second advent, of Christ.

It will, of course, be clearly understood that the Scriptures which speak of His visible and bodily appearing at the close of this dispensation must be distinguished from those which refer to His divine attributes of omniscience and omnipresence, by virtue of which He knows all things and is always present everywhere and of which such passages as Matthew 18:20 and Matthew 28:20 are examples. It is blessedly true that, in this sense, He is with us always, even unto the end of the age.

But the man Christ Jesus is now personally and corporeally at the right hand of God, as Acts 1:9-11 plainly declares: "And when he had spoken these things, while they beheld, he was taken up and a cloud received him out of their sight. And while they looked steadfastly toward heaven as he went up, behold, two men stood by them in white apparel; which also said, Ye men of Galilee, why stand ye gazing up into heaven? this same Jesus, which is taken up from you into heaven, shall so come in like manner as ye have seen him go into heaven."

Stephen saw Him there: "But he, being full of the Holy Ghost looked up steadfastly into heaven, and saw the glory of God, and Jesus standing on the right hand of God, and said, Behold, I see the heavens opened, and the Son of man standing on the right hand of God" (Acts 7:55-56). "When he had by himself purged our sins, sat down on the right hand of the Majesty on high" (Heb. 1:3). "If ye then be risen with Christ, seek those things which are above, where Christ sitteth on the right hand of God" (Col. 3: 1).

During the Franco-Prussian war Von Moltke, by his genius and skill and by a network of telegraph wires, was really present on every battlefield, though visibly and personally present in his office in Berlin. Later in the war he joined the army before Paris, after which his actual and visible presence was there. So our Lord, by virtue of His divine attributes, is really present with His church now, but He will be visibly and personally upon the earth at His second coming.

1. The prophecies concerning the return of the Lord were not fulfilled by the descent of the Holy Spirit at Pentecost, nor by His manifestation in powerful revivals and happy prayer meetings.

a. This interpretation practically nullifies the doctrine of the Trinity, making the Holy Spirit only a manifestation of Christ.

b. In Christ's promise of the descent of the Spirit He distinctly speaks of Him as "another Comforter" (John 14:16), and in John 16:7 Christ says: "If I go not away, the Comforter will not come unto you; but if I depart I will send him unto you."

c. The inspired writers of Acts, the Epistles, and of Revelation, mention the return of the Lord more than one hundred and fifty times after Pentecost, and always as yet future.

d. None of the events predicted to accompany the second advent of Christ occurred at Pentecost. These are: the resurrection of sleeping saints (I Cor. 15:22-23; 1 Thess. 4:13-16), the "change" of living believers, by which they "put on incorruption", their vile bodies" being "fashioned like unto His glorious body," and their being caught up to meet the Lord in the air (I Cor. 15:51-53; 1 Thess. 4:17; Phil. 3:20-21), and the mourning of all the tribes of the earth because of the visible coming of the Son of man in power and great glory (Matt. 24:29-30; Rev. 1:7).

These are the phenomena associated with the event of our Lord's return. When He comes, these phenomena will be present. Not one of these things occurred at Pentecost, nor in any other manifestation of the Holy Spirit.

2. The conversion of a sinner is not the coming of the Lord.
One would think this theory too puerile to be seriously put forth as a sufficient explanation of prophecies so numerous and circumstantial.

a. According to Scripture this is exactly reversed. Conversion is the coming of a sinner to Christ, not the coming of Christ to a sinner (Matt. 11:28; John 5:40; John 7:37; John 6:37).

b. None of the events enumerated above, predicted to occur when the Lord returns, accompany the conversion of a sinner.

3. The death of a Christian is not the coming of Christ.
a. When the disciples understood the Lord to say that one of their number should tarry till He came, the saying went abroad among them that "that disciple should not die" (John 21:22-24).

b. The inspired writers always refer to a believer's death as his departure. In not one instance is the coming of the Lord connected with a Christian's death. (See Phil. 1:23; 2 Tim. 4:6; 2 Cor. 5:8.) Dying Stephen saw the heavens opened, and the Son of man, not coming but "standing on the right hand of God" (Acts 7:55-56).

c. None of the events predicted to occur when the Lord returns accompany the death of a Christian.

4. The destruction of Jerusalem by the Romans was not the second coming of Christ.

a. In Matthew 24 and Luke 21 three events are foretold: the destruction of the temple, the coming of the Lord, and the end of the world (age). (See Matt. 24:3.) It was the needless confusion of these perfectly distinct things which gave rise to the notion that the fulfillment of one was the fulfillment of all.

b. The apostle John wrote the book of Revelation after the destruction of Jerusalem, but still speaks of the coming of the Lord as a future event (Rev. 1:4,7; 2:25; 3:11; 22:7,12,20). The last promise of the Bible is, "Surely, I come quickly"; the last prayer, "Even so, come Lord Jesus."

c. None of the events predicted to occur when the Lord returns occurred when Jerusalem was destroyed. (See I Thess. 4:14-17 Matt. 24:29-31; Matt. 25:31-32.)

5. The diffusion of Christianity is not the second coming of Christ.

a. The diffusion of Christianity is gradual, whereas the Scriptures refer to the return of the Lord as sudden and unexpected (Matt. 24:27, 36-42, 44, 50; 2 Pet. 3:10; Rev. 3:3).

b. The diffusion of Christianity is a process; Scripture invariably speaks of the return of the Lord as an event.

c. The diffusion of Christianity brings salvation to the wicked, whereas the coming of Christ is said to bring not salvation to them but "sudden destruction" (I Thess. 5:2, 3; 2 Thess. 1:7-10; Matt. 25:31- 46).

6. These alleged explanations and theories, though widespread, do not appear in the books of reputable theologians of any school or denomination, nor are they maintained by a single exegete of universally recognized eminence. These all maintain the bodily and visible second coming of Christ. It is, however, sometimes said that this coming cannot occur until after the world has been converted by the preaching of the gospel and has submitted to the spiritual reign of Christ for one thousand years. It is submitted that this view is wholly erroneous for the following reasons.

a. Scripture clearly describes the condition of the earth at the second coming of Christ to be one of awful wickedness, not of millennial blessedness (Luke 17:26-32, with Gen. 6:5-7 and Gen. 13:13; Luke 18:8; Luke 21:25-27).

b. Scripture describes the whole course of this dispensation from the beginning to the end in such terms as to exclude the possibility of a converted world in any part of it (Matt. 13:36-43, 47-50; Matt. 25: 1 - 10; 1 Tim. 4: 1; 2 Tim. 3:1-9; 4:3-4; 2 Pet. 3:3-4; Jude 17-19).

c. The purpose of God in this dispensation is declared to be to "gather out of the Gentiles a people for his name," not the conversion of the world. After this He "will return," and then, and not before, will the world be converted. (See Acts 15:14-17; Matt. 24:14 ["for a witness"]; Rom. 1:5 ["among" not "of" all nations]; Rom. 11:14 ["some," not "all"]; I Cor. 9:22; Rev. 5:9 ["out of" not "all" of].)

d. It would be impossible to "watch" and "wait" for an event which we knew could not occur for more than one thousand years.

Chapter 4
THE TWO RESURRECTIONS

The Word of truth teaches in the clearest and most positive terms that all of the dead will be raised. No doctrine of the faith rests upon a more literal and emphatic body of Scripture authority than this, nor is any more vital to Christianity. "But if there be no resurrection of the dead, then is Christ not risen. And if Christ be not risen, then is our preaching vain, and your faith is also vain" (I Cor. 15:13-14.)

But it is important to observe that the Scriptures do not teach that all the dead are raised at one time. A partial resurrection of saints has already occurred. "And the graves were opened; and many bodies of the saints which slept arose, and came out of the graves after his resurrection, and went into the holy city, and appeared unto many" (Matt. 27:52-53).

Two resurrections, differing in respect of time and of those who are the subjects of the resurrection, are yet future. These are variously distinguished as "the resurrection of life," and "the resurrection of damnation," "the resurrection of the just and the unjust," etc. The following Scriptures refer to this important subject.

"Marvel not at this: for the hour is coming, in the which all that are in the graves shall hear his voice, and shall come forth; they that have done good, unto the resurrection of life; and they that have done evil, unto the resurrection of damnation" (John 5:28-29.) If it be objected that the word "hour" would indicate a simultaneous resurrection of these two classes, it is answered that the "hour" of verse 25 has already lasted eighteen hundred years. (See also "day," in 2 Pet. 3:8; 2 Cor. 6:2; John 8:56).

"But when thou makest a feast, call the poor, the maimed, the lame, the blind: and thou shalt be blessed; for they cannot recompense thee: for thou shalt be recompensed at the resurrection of the just" (Luke 14:13-14). In this passage our Lord speaks of the first resurrection only. In I Corinthians 15 the distinction still further appears: "For as in Adam all die, even so in Christ shall all be made alive. But every man in his own order: Christ the firstfruits; afterward they that are Christ's at his coming" (I Cor. 15:22-23).

"But I would not have you to be ignorant, brethren, concerning them which are asleep, that ye sorrow not, even as others which have no hope. For if we believe that Jesus died and rose again, even so them also which sleep in Jesus will God bring with him. For this we say unto you by the word of the Lord, that we which are alive and remain unto the coming of the Lord, shall not prevent (precede] them which are asleep. For the Lord himself shall descend from heaven with a shout, with the voice of the archangel, and with the trump of God: and the dead in Christ shall rise first" (I Thess. 4:13-16).

If the apostle had in mind a resurrection of all the dead, how could he speak of attaining it "by any means," since he could not possibly escape it?

In Revelation 20:4-6 the two resurrections are again mentioned together, with the important addition of the time which intervenes between the resurrection of the saved and of the unsaved. "And I saw thrones, and they sat upon them, and judgment was given unto them: and I saw the souls of them that were beheaded for the witness of Jesus, and for the word of God, and which had not worshipped the Beast neither his image, neither had received his mark upon their foreheads, or in their hands; and they lived and reigned with Christ a thousand years. But the rest of the dead lived not again until the thousand years were finished. This is the first resurrection. Blessed and holy is he that hath part in the first resurrection: on such the second death hath no power, but they shall be priests of God and of Christ, and shall reign with him a thousand years." Verses 12 and 13 describe the second resurrection-that "unto damnation."

The testimony of Scripture, then, is clear that believers' bodies are raised from among the bodies of unbelievers and caught up to meet the Lord in the air a thousand years before the resurrection of the latter. It should be firmly held that the doctrine of the resurrection concerns only the bodies of the dead. Their disembodied spirits are instantly in conscious bliss or woe (Phil. 1:23 2 Con 5.8; Luke 16:22-23).

Chapter 5
THE FIVE JUDGMENTS

The expression "general judgment," of such frequent occurrence in religious literature, is not found in the Scriptures, and, what is of more importance, the idea intended to be conveyed by that expression is not found in the Scriptures.

The Scriptures speak of five judgments, and they differ in four general respects: as to who are the subjects of judgment; as to the place of judgment; as to the time of judgment; as to the result of the judgment.

THE JUDGMENT AS TO BELIEVERS

Their sins have been judged.

Time: A. D. 30.

Place: the cross.

Result: death for Christ: justification for the believer.

'And he bearing his cross went forth into a place called the place of a skull, which is called in the Hebrew, Golgotha: Where they crucified him" (John 19:17-18).

"Who his own self bare our sins in his own body on the tree" I Pet. 2:24).

"For Christ also hath once suffered for sins, the just for the unjust, that he might bring us to God" (I Pet. 3: 18).

"Christ hath redeemed us from the curse of the law, being made a curse for us: for it is written, Cursed is every one that hangeth on a tree" (Gal. 3:13).

"For he [God] hath made him [Christ] to be sin for us, who knew no sin; that we might be made the righteousness of God in him" (2 Cor. 5:21).

"But now once in the end of the world hath he appeared, to put away sin by the sacrifice of himself" (Heb. 9:26).

"When he had by himself purged our sins" (Heb. 1:3).

"There is therefore now no condemnation to them which are in Christ Jesus, who walk not after the flesh, but after the Spirit." (Rom. 8:1).

THE JUDGMENT OF SIN IN THE BELIEVER

Time: any time.

Place: anywhere.

Result: chastisement by the Lord, if we judge not ourselves.

"For if we would judge ourselves, we should not be judged. But when we are judged, we are chastened of the Lord, that we should not be condemned with the world" (I Cor. 11:31-32).

"If ye endure chastening, God dealeth with you as with sons; for what son is he whom the father chasteneth not?" (Heb. 12:7).

(See also I Pet. 4:17; 1 Cor. 5:5; 2 Sam. 7:14-15; 2 Sam. 12:13-14; 1 Tim. 1:20.)

THE CONDUCT, OR WORKS OF BELIEVERS ARE TO BE JUDGED

Time: when Christ comes.

Place: "in the air."

Result to the believer: "reward" or "loss." "But he himself shall be saved." It is a solemn thought that though Christ bore our sins in Hi own body on the tree and God has entered into covenant with us to "remember them no more" (Heb. 10: 17), every work must corn into judgment. The life, the works of the believer must be reviewed by the Lord.

"Wherefore we labour, that, whether present or absent, we may be accepted of him. For we must all appear before the judgment seat of Christ; that every one may receive the things done in his body, according to that he hath done, whether it be good or bad." (2 Cor. 5:9-10).

"But why dost thou judge thy brother? or why dost thou set a naught thy brother? for we shall all stand before the judgment seat of Christ" (Rom. 14: 10).

It will be observed that both of these passages are limited by the context to believers. In the first, the apostle speaks of us as in one of two states: either we are at home in the body and absen from the Lord, or absent from the body and present with the Lord-language which could not he used of unbelievers. "Where fore we make it our aim" to be well-pleasing unto the Lord, 'fio we must all be made manifest" (2 Cor. 5:8-9).

In the other passage the words "we" and "brother" again limi it to believers. The Holy Spirit never comingles the saved and the unsaved. Then, lest it should seem incredible that a blood-cleansed saint could come into any judgment whatever, he quotes from Isaiah to prove that "every knee shall bow," and adds, "So then every one of us shall give account of himself to God."

The following passage gives the basis of the judgment of works: "For other foundation can no man lay than that is laid, which is Jesus Christ. Now if any man build upon this foundation gold, silver, precious stones, wood, hay, stubble: every man's work shall be made manifest: for the day shall declare it, because it shall be revealed by fire; and the fire shall try every man's work of what sort it is. If any man's work abide which he hath built thereupon, he shall receive a reward. If any man's work shall be burned, he shall suffer loss; but he himself shall be saved; yet so as by fire" (I Cor. 3:11-15).

The following passages fix the time of this judgment: "For the Son of man shall come in the glory of his Father, with his angels: and then he shall reward every man according to his works" (Matt. 16:27). "And thou shalt be blessed; for they cannot recompense thee: for thou shalt be recompensed at the resurrection of the just" (Luke 14:14). (See I Cor. 15:22-23.) "Therefore judge nothing before the time, until the Lord come, who both will bring to light the hidden things of darkness, and will make manifest the counsels of the hearts: and then shall every man have praise of God" (I Cor. 4:5).

But how comforting it is, in view of that inevitable scrutiny of our poor works, to learn that in His patient love He is so leading us and working in us now that He can then find something in it all for which to praise us.

"Behold, I come quickly; and my reward is with me, to give every man according as his work shall be" (Rev. 22:12).

"Henceforth there is laid up for me a crown of righteousness, which the Lord, the righteous Judge, shall give me at that day" (2 Tim. 4:9).

For the place of this judgment, see I Thessalonians 4:17 and Matthew 25:24-30.

THE JUDGMENT OF THE NATIONS

Time: the glorious appearing of Christ (Matt. 25:31-32; Matt. 13:40-41).

Place: the valley of Jehoshaphat (Joel 3:1-2,12-14).

Result: some saved, some lost (Matt. 25:46).
Basis: The treatment of those whom Christ there calls, "my brethren" (Matt. 25:40-45; Joel 3:3,6- 7). These "brethren" we believe are the Jewish remnant who shall turn to Jesus as their Messiah during "the great tribulation" which follows the taking away of the church and is terminated by the glorious appearing of our Lord (Matt. 24:21-22; Rev. 7:14; 2 Thess. 2:3-9). The proof is too extensive to be put forth here. It is evident, however, that these "brethren" cannot be believers of this dispensation, for it would be impossible to find any considerable number of Christians who are so ignorant that they do not know that offices of kindness to believers are really ministries to Jesus Himself.

As this judgment of the living nations is sometimes confounded with that of the great white throne in Revelation 20:11, it may be well to note the following contrasts between the two scenes.

The living nations will be characterized by the following: no resurrection; living nations judged; on the earth; no books; three classes-sheep, goats, "brethren"; time, when Christ appears. The great white throne will be characterized by the following: a resurrection; "the dead" judged; heavens and earth fled away; "books were opened"; one class: "the dead"; after He has reigned one thousand years.

The saints will be associated with Christ in this judgment and hence cannot be the subjects of it. (See I Cor. 6:2; Dan. 7:22; Jude verses 14-15.)

In truth, the judgment of the great white throne and the judgment of the living nations have but one thing in common: the Judge.

THE JUDGMENT OF THE WICKED DEAD

Time: a determined day, after the millennium (Acts 17:31; Rev. 20:5,7).

Place: before the great white throne (Rev. 20: 11

Result: Rev. 20:15.

Some may be troubled by the word "day" in such passages as Acts 17:31 and in Romans 2:16. See the following passages, where "day" means a lengthened period: 2 Pet. 3:8; 2 Cor. 6:2; John 8:56. The "hour" of John 5:25 has now lasted more than eighteen hundred years.

The Scriptures speak, also, of a judgment of angels (I Cor. 6:3; Jude verse 6; 2 Pet. 2:4). Luke 22:30 probably refers to judges as under the theocracy - an administrative office, rather than judicial. (See Isaiah 1:26.)

Chapter 6
LAW AND GRACE

The most obvious and striking division of the Word of truth is that between law and grace. Indeed, these contrasting principles characterize the two most important dispensations: the Jewish and Christian. "For the law was given by Moses, but grace and truth came by Jesus Christ" (John 1:17).

It is not, of course, meant that there was no law before Moses, any more than that there was no grace and truth before Jesus Christ. The forbidding to Adam of the fruit of the tree of the knowledge of good and evil (Gen. 2:17) was law, and surely grace was most sweetly manifested in the Lord God seeking His sinning creatures and in His clothing them with coats of skins (Gen. 3:21)-a beautiful type of Christ who "is made unto us . . . righteousness" (1 Cor. 1:30). Law, in the sense of some revelation of God's will, and grace, in the sense of some revelation of God's goodness, have always existed, and to this Scripture abundantly testifies. But "the law" most frequently mentioned in Scripture was given by Moses, and from Sinai to Calvary, dominates, characterizes, the time; just as grace dominates or gives its peculiar character to the dispensation which begins at Calvary and has its predicted termination in the rapture of the church.

It is, however, of the most vital moment to observe that Scripture never, in any dispensation, mingles these two principles. Law always has a place and work distinct and wholly diverse from that of grace. Law is God prohibiting and requiring; grace is God beseeching and bestowing. Law is a ministry of condemnation; grace, of forgiveness. Law curses; grace redeems from that curse. Law kills; grace makes alive. Law shuts every mouth before God; grace opens every mouth to praise Him. Law puts a great and guilty distance between man and God; grace makes guilty man nigh to God. Law says, 'An eye for an eye, and a tooth for a tooth"; grace says, "Resist not evil: but whosoever shall smite thee on thy right cheek, turn to him the other also." Law says, "Hate thine enemy"; grace says, "Love your enemies, bless them that despitefully use you." Law says, do and live; grace says, believe and live. Law never had a missionary; grace is to be preached to every creature. Law utterly condemns the best man; grace freely justifies the worst (Luke 23:43; Rom. 5:8; 1 Tim 1:15; 1 Cor. 6:9-11). Law is a system of probation; grace, of favor. Law stones an adulteress; grace says, "Neither do I condemn thee: go, and sin no more." Under law the sheep dies for the shepherd: under grace the Shepherd dies for the sheep.

Everywhere the Scriptures present law and grace in sharply contrasted spheres. The mingling of them in much of the current teaching of the day spoils both, for law is robbed of its terror, and grace of its freeness.

The student should observe that "law" in the New Testament Scriptures, means the law given by Moses (Rom. 7:23 is an exception). Sometimes the entire law (the moral, or the Ten Commandments and the ceremonial) is meant; sometimes the commandments only; sometimes the ceremonial only. Among passages of the first type, Romans 6:14; Galatians 2:16, and 3:2 are examples. Of the second type, Romans 3:19 and 7:7-12 are examples. Of the third type, Colossians 2:14-17 is an example.

It should be remembered also that in the ceremonial law are enshrined those marvelous types-the beautiful foreshadowings of the person and work of the Lord Jesus as priest and sacrifice, as in the tabernacle (Exod. 25-30) and levitical offerings (Lev. 1-7), which must ever be the wonder and delight of the spiritually minded.

Expressions in the Psalms too, which would be inexplicable if understood only of the "ministration of death, written and engraven in stones" (2 Cor. 3:7), are made clear when seen to refer to Christ or to the redeemed. "But his delight is in the law of the LORD; and in his law doth he meditate day and night" (Ps. 1:2). "O how I love thy law! It is my meditation all the day" (Ps. 119:97).

Three errors have troubled the church concerning the right relation of law to grace:

1. **Antinomianism**- the denial of all rule over the lives of believers; the affirmation that men are not required to live holy lives because they are saved by God's free grace, "They profess that they know God; but in works they deny him, being abominable, and disobedient, and unto every good work reprobate" (Titus 1: 16).

"For there are certain men crept in unawares, who were before of old ordained to this condemnation; ungodly men, turning the grace of our God into lasciviousness, and denying the only Lord God, and our Lord Jesus Christ" (Jude verse 4).

2. **Ceremonialism**- the demand that believers should observe the levitical ordinances. The modern form of this error is the teaching that Christian ordinances are essential to salvation.

"And certain men which came down from Judaea taught the brethren, and said, Except ye be circumcised after the manner of Moses, ye cannot be saved" (Acts 15:1).

3. **Galatianism**- the mingling of law and grace; the teaching that justification is partly by grace, partly by law, or, that grace is given to enable an otherwise helpless sinner to keep the law. Against this error, the most wide-spread of all, the solemn warnings, the. unanswerable logic, the emphatic declarations of the Epistle to the Galatians are God's conclusive answer.

"This only would I learn of you, Received ye the Spirit by the works of the law, or by the hearing of faith? Are ye so foolish? having begun in the Spirit, are ye now made perfect by the flesh?" (Gal. 3:2- 3).

"I marvel that ye are so soon removed from him that called you into the grace of Christ unto another gospel: which is not another [there could not be another gospel]; but there be some that trouble you, and would pervert the gospel of Christ. But though we, or an angel from heaven, preach any other gospel unto you than that which we have preached unto you, let him be accursed" (Gal. 1:6-8).

The following may be helpful as an outline of Scripture teaching on this important subject. The moral law only is referred to in the passages cited.

WHAT THE LAW IS

"Wherefore the law is holy, and the commandment holy, and just, and good" (Rom. 7:12),

"For we know that the law is spiritual: but I am carnal, sold under sin" (Rom. 7:14).

"For I delight in the law of God after the inward man" (Rom. 7:22).

"But we know that the law is good, if a man use it lawfully" (I Tim. 1:8).

"And the law is not of faith" (Gal. 3:12).

THE LAWFUL USE OF THE LAW

"What shall we say then? Is the law sin? God forbid. Nay, I had not known sin, but by the law: for I had not known lust, except the law had said, Thou shalt not covet" (Rom. 7:7; see also verse 13).

"Therefore by the deeds of the law there shall no flesh be justified in his sight: for by the law is the knowledge of sin" (Rom. 3:20).

"Wherefore then serveth the law? It was added because Of transgressions" (Gal. 3:19).

"Now we know, that what things soever the law saith, it saith to them who are under the law; that every mouth may be stopped, and all the world may become guilty before God" (Rom. 3:19). Law has but one language: "what things soever." It speaks only to condemn.

"For as many as are of the works of the law are under the curse: for it is written, Cursed is every one that continueth not in all things which are written in the book of the law to do them" (Gal. 3: 10).

"For whosoever shall keep the whole law, and yet offend in one point, he is guilty of all" (James 2:10).

"The ministration of death, written and engraven in stones" (2 Cor. 3:7).

"The ministration of condemnation" (2 Cor. 3:9).

"For I was alive without the law once: but when the commandment came, sin revived, and I died" (Rom. 7:9).

"The strength of sin is the law" (1 Cor. 15:56).

"It is evident, then, that God's purpose in giving the law, after the race had existed twenty-five hundred years without it (John 1: 17; Gal. 3:17), was to bring to guilty man the knowledge of his sin first, and then of his utter helplessness in view of God's just requirements. It is purely and only a ministration of condemnation and death.

WHAT THE LAW CANNOT DO

"Therefore by the deeds of the law there shall no flesh be justified in his sight: for by the law is the knowledge of sin" (Rom. 3:20).

"Knowing that a man is not justified by the works of the law, but by the faith of Jesus Christ, even we have believed in Jesus Christ, that we might be justified by the faith of Christ, and not by the works of the law: for by the works of the law shall no flesh be justified" (Gal. 2:16).

"I do not frustrate the grace of God: for if righteousness come by the law, then Christ is dead in vain" (Gal. 2:21).

"But that no man is justified by the law in the sight of God, it is evident: for, the just shall live by faith" (Gal. 3: 11).

"For what the law could not do, in that it was weak through the flesh, God, sending his own Son in the likeness of sinful flesh, and for sin, condemned sin in the flesh" (Rom. 8:3).

"And by him, all that believe are justified from all things, from which ye could not be justified by the law of Moses" (Acts 13:39).

"For the law made nothing perfect, but the bringing in of a better hope did; by the which we draw nigh unto God" (Heb. 7:19).

THE BELIEVER IS NOT UNDER THE LAW

Romans 6, after declaring the doctrine of the believer's identification with Christ in His death, of which baptism is the symbol (verses 1-10), begins, with verse 11, the declarations of the principles which should govern the walk of the believer-his rule of life. This is the subject of the remaining twelve verses. Verse 14 gives the great principle of his deliverance, not from the guilt of sin that is met by Christ's blood, but from the dominion of sin-his bondage* under it. "For sin shall not have dominion over you: for ye are not under the law, but under grace."

Lest this should lead to the monstrous Antinomianism of saying that therefore a godly life was not important, the Spirit immediately adds: "What then? Shall we sin, because we are not under the law, but under grace? God forbid" (Rom.

6:15). Surely every renewed heart answers 'Amen" to this.

Then Romans 7 introduces another principle of deliverance from law. "Wherefore, my brethren, ye also are become dead to the law by the body of Christ; that ye should he married to another, even to him who is raised from the dead, that we should bring forth fruit unto God. For when we were in the flesh, the motions of sins, which were by the law, did work in our members to bring forth fruit unto death. But now we are delivered from the law, that being dead wherein we were held; that we should serve in newness of spirit, and not in the oldness of the letter" (Rom. 7:4-6). (This does not refer to the ceremonial law; see verse 7.)

"For I through the law am dead to the law, that I might live unto God" (Gal. 2:19).

"But before faith came, we were kept under the law, shut up, unto the faith which should afterwards be revealed. Wherefore the law was our schoolmaster to bring us unto Christ, that we might be justified by faith. But after that faith is come, we are no longer under a schoolmaster" (Gal. 3:23-25).

"But we know that the law is good, if a man use it lawfully; knowing this, that the law is not made for a righteous man" (I Tim. 1:8-9).
WHAT IS THE BELIEVER'S RULE OF LIFE?
"He that saith he abideth in him, ought himself also so to walk, even as he walked" (I John 2:6).

"Hereby perceive we the love of God, because he laid down his life for us: and we ought to lay down our lives for the brethren" (I John 3:16).

"Dearly beloved, I beseech you as strangers and pilgrims, abstain from fleshly lusts, which war against the soul" (I Pet. 2:11; see also verses 12-23).

"I therefore, the prisoner of the Lord, beseech you that ye walk worthy of the vocation wherewith ye are called, with all lowliness and meekness, with long-suffering, forbearing one another in love" (Eph. 4:1-2).

"Be ye therefore followers of God, as dear children; and walk in love as Christ also hath loved us, and hath given himself for us" (Eph. 5:1-2).

"For ye were sometimes darkness, but now are ye light in the Lord: walk as children of light" (Eph. 5:8).

"See then that ye walk circumspectly, not as fools, but as wise, redeeming the time, because the days are evil" (Eph. 5:15-16).

"This I say then, Walk in the Spirit, and ye shall not fulfil the lust of the flesh" (Gal. 5:16).

"For I have given you an example, that ye should do as I have, done to you" (John 13:15).

"If ye keep my commandments, ye shall abide in my love; even as I have kept my Father's commandments, and abide in his love" (John 15: 10).

"This is my commandment, That ye love one another, as I have loved you" (John 15:12).

"He that hath my commandments, and keepeth them, he it is that loveth me" (John 14:21).

'And whatsoever we ask, we receive of him, because we keep his commandments, and do those things that are pleasing in his sight. And this is his commandment, That we should believe on the name of his Son Jesus Christ, and love one another, as he gave us commandment" (I John 3:22-23).

"This is the covenant that I will make with them after those days, saith the Lord; I will put my laws into their hearts, and in their minds will I write them" (Heb. 10: 16).

A beautiful illustration of this principle is seen in a mother's love for her child. The law requires parents to care for their offspring and pronounces penalties for the willful neglect of them; but the land is full of happy mothers who tenderly care for their children in perfect ignorance of the existence of such a statute. The law is in their hearts.

It is instructive, in this connection, to remember that God's appointed place for the tables of the law was within the ark of the testimony. With them were "the golden pot that had manna, and Aaron's rod that budded" (types: the one of Christ our wilderness bread, the other of resurrection, and both speaking of grace), while they were covered from sight by the golden mercy seat upon which was sprinkled the blood of atonement. The eye of God could see His broken law only through the blood that completely vindicated His justice and propitiated His wrath (Heb. 9:4-5).

It was reserved to modernists to wrench these holy and just but deathful tables from underneath the mercy seat and the atoning blood and erect them in Christian churches as the rule of Christian life.

WHAT IS GRACE?

"But after that the kindness and love of God our Saviour toward man appeared . . . according to his mercy he saved us" (Titus 3:4-5). "That in the ages to come he might show the exceeding riches of his grace, in his kindness toward us through Christ Jesus" (Eph. 2:7).

"But God commendeth his love toward us, in that, while we were yet sinners, Christ died for us" (Rom. 5:8).

WHAT IS GOD'S PURPOSE IN GRACE?

"For by grace are ye saved through faith; and that not of yourselves; it is the gift of God: not of works, lest any man should boast" (Eph. 2:8-9).

"For the grace of God that bringeth salvation hath appeared to all men, teaching us that, denying ungodliness and worldly lusts, we should live soberly, righteously, and godly, in this present world: looking for that blessed hope, and the glorious appearing of the great God and our Saviour Jesus Christ" (Titus 2:11-13).

"That, being justified by his grace, we should be made heirs according to the hope of eternal life" (Titus 3:7).

"Being justified freely by his grace; through the redemption that is in Christ Jesus" (Rom. 3:24).

"By whom also we have access by faith into this grace wherein we stand" (Rom. 5:2).

"And now, brethren, I commend you to God, and to the word of his grace, which is able to build you up, and to give you an inheritance among all them which are sanctified" (Acts 20:32).

"To the praise of the glory of his grace, wherein he hath made us accepted in the beloved: in whom we have redemption through f. his blood, the forgiveness of sins, according to the riches of his grace" (Eph. 1:6-7).

"Let us therefore come boldly unto the throne of grace, that we may obtain mercy, and find grace to help in time of need"(Heb. 4:16).

"How complete, how all-inclusive! Grace saves, justifies, builds up, makes accepted, redeems, forgives, bestows an inheritance, gives standing before God, provides a throne of grace to which we may come boldly for mercy and help; it teaches us how to live and gives us a blessed hope! It remains to note that these diverse principles cannot be intermingled.

"And if by grace, then is it no more of works: otherwise grace is no more grace. But if it be of works, then is it no more grace: otherwise work is no more work" (Rom. 11:6).

"Now to him that worketh is the reward not reckoned of grace, but of debt. But to him that worketh not, but believeth on him that justifieth the ungodly, his faith is counted for righteousness" (Rom. 4:4-5; see also Gal. 3:16-18; 4:21-31).

"So then, brethren, we are not children of the bond-woman, but of the free" (Gal. 4:31).

"For ye are not come unto the mount that might be touched, and that burned with fire, nor unto blackness, and darkness, and tempest, and the sound of a trumpet, and the voice of words: which voice they that heard entreated that the word should not be spoken to them any more (for they could not endure that which was commanded, And if so much as a beast touch the mountain, it shall he stoned, or thrust through with a dart: and so terrible was the sight, that Moses said, I exceedingly fear and quake). But ye are come unto Mount Sion, and unto the city of the living God, the heavenly Jerusalem, and to an innumerable company of angels, to the general assembly and church of the firstborn which are written in heaven, and to God the judge of all, and to the spirits of just men made perfect, and to Jesus the mediator of the new covenant, and to the blood of sprinkling, that speaketh better things than that of Abel" (Heb. 12:18-24).

It is not, then a question of dividing what God spoke from Sinai into moral law and ceremonial law-the believer does not come to that mount at all.

As sound old Bunyan said: "The believer is now, by faith in the Lord Jesus, shrouded under so perfect and blessed a righteousness, that this thundering law of Mount Sinai cannot find the least fault or diminution therein. This is called the righteousness of God without the law."

Should this meet the eye of an unbeliever, he is affectionately exhorted to accept the true sentence of that holy and just law which he has violated: "For there is no difference: for all have sinned, and come short of the glory of God" (Rom. 3:22-23). In Christ such will find a perfect and eternal salvation, as it is written: "If thou shalt confess with thy mouth the Lord Jesus, and shalt believe in thine heart that God hath raised him from the dead, thou shalt be saved" (Rom. 10:9); for Christ is "the end of the law for righteousness to every one that believeth" (Rom. 10:4).

Chapter 7
THE BELIEVER'S TWO NATURES

The Scriptures teach that every regenerate person is the possessor of two natures: one, received by natural birth, which is wholly and hopelessly bad; and a new nature, received through the new birth, which is the nature of God Himself, and therefore wholly good.

The following Scriptures will sufficiently manifest what God thinks of the old, or Adam nature: "Behold, I was shapen in iniquity, and in sin did my mother conceive me" (Ps. 51:5).

"The heart is deceitful above all things, and desperately wicked: who can know it?" (Jer. 17:9)

"There is none righteous, no, not one: there is none that understandeth, there is none that seeketh after God. They are all gone out of the way, they are together become unprofitable; there is none that doeth good, no, not one" (Rom. 3:10-12).

God does not say that none of the unregenerate are refined, or cultured, or able, or sweet-tempered, or generous, or charitable, or even religious. But He does say that none are righteous, none understand God, or seek after Him.

It is one of the sorest of faith's trials to accept the divine estimate of human nature, to realize that our genial and moral friends, who, not infrequently, are scrupulous in the discharge of every duty, filled with sympathy for the woes and the aspirations of humanity, and strenuous in the assertion of human rights, are yet utter despisers of God's rights and untouched by the sacrifice of His Son, whose divinity they with unspeakable insolence deny and whose word they contemptuously reject. A refined and gentle lady who would shrink with horror from the coarseness of giving a fellow creature the lie, will yet make God a liar every day! (See I John 1:10; 5:10). And this difficulty is vastly increased for thousands by the current praise of humanity from the pulpit.

How startling the contrast between appearances and realities in the time before the flood. "There were giants in the earth in those days; and also after that, when the sons of God came in unto the daughters of men, and they bare children to them, the same became mighty men which were of old, men of renown" (Gen. 6:4).

And so it appeared that the world was growing better, in men's eyes; a continual improvement they probably would trace, and the apparent result of the unholy intermarriage of the godly with the worldly was the lifting up of human nature to still grander heights.

But "God saw that the wickedness of man was great in the earth, and that every imagination of the thoughts of his heart was only evil continually" (Gen. 6:5).

"For from within, out of the heart of men, proceed evil thoughts, adulteries, fornications, murders, thefts, covetousness, wickedness, deceit, lasciviousness, an evil eye, blasphemy, pride, foolishness: all these evil things come from within, and defile man" (Mark 7:21-23).

"But the natural man receiveth not the things of the Spirit of God: for they are foolishness unto him: neither can he know them, because they are spiritually discerned" (I Cor. 2:14).

"Because the carnal mind is enmity against God; for it is not subject to the law of God, neither indeed can be. So then they that are in the flesh cannot please God" (Rom. 8:7-8).

"Among whom also we all had our conversation in times past in the lusts of our flesh, fulfilling the desires of the flesh and of the mind; and were by nature the children of wrath" (Eph. 2:3).

By these it appears that the unconverted man has a three-fold incapacity. He may be gifted, or cultured, or amiable, or generous, or religious. He may pay his honest debts, be truthful, industrious, a good husband and father-or all these together-but he can neither obey God, please God, nor understand God.

The believer, on the contrary, while still having his old nature, unchanged and unchangeable, has received a new nature which "after God is created in righteousness and true holiness." The following Scriptures will show the origin and character of the new man.

It will be seen that regeneration is a creation, not a mere transformation-the bringing in a new thing, not the change of an old. As we received human nature by natural generation, so do we receive the divine nature by regeneration.

"Verily, verily, I say unto thee [Nicodemus, a moral, religious man], Except a man be born again, he cannot see the kingdom of God" (John 3:3).

"But as many as received him, to them gave he power to become the sons of God, even to them that believe on his name: which were born, not of blood, nor of the will of the flesh, nor of the will of man, but of God" (John 1:12-13).

"For ye are all the children of God by faith in Christ Jesus" (Gal. 3:26).

It will be observed what bearing these Scriptures have upon that specious and plausible, but utterly unscriptural phrase so popular in our day, "the universal fatherhood of God, and the universal brotherhood of man -- an expression all the more dangerous for the half-truth of the last clause. Not all who are born, but all who are born again are the children of God. The Scripture tells us indeed that Adam was the son of God, but it is also careful to state that Seth was the son of Adam (Luke 3:38).

"And that ye put on the new man, which after God is created in righteousness and true holiness" (Eph. 4:24).

"Therefore if any man be in Christ, he is a new creature [literally, a new creation]: old things are passed away; behold, all things are become new" (2 Cor. 5:17).

And this "new man" is linked with Christ. "I am crucified with Christ: nevertheless I live; yet not 1, but Christ liveth in me: and the life which I now live in the flesh, I live by the faith of the Son of God, who loved me and gave himself for me" (Gal. 2:20).

"To whom God would make known what is the riches of the glory of this mystery among the Gentiles; which is Christ in you, the hope of glory" (Col. 1:27).

"For ye are dead, and your life is hid with Christ in God. When Christ who is our life shall appear, then shall ye also appear with him in glory" (Col. 3:3-4).

"Whereby are given unto us exceeding great and precious promises; that by these ye might be partakers of the divine nature" (2 Pet. 1:4).

And if Christ be in you, the body is dead because of sin; but the Spirit is life because of righteousness" (Rom. 8: 10).

"And this is the record, that God hath given to us eternal life, and this life is in his Son. He that hath the Son hath life: and he that hath not the Son of God hath not life" (I John 5:11-12).

"But this new, divine nature, which is Christ's own, subsists in the believer together with the old nature. It is the same Paul who could say, "Yet not I, but Christ liveth in me," who also says, "For I know that in me (that is, in my flesh), dwelleth no good thing" (Rom. 7: 18); and, "I find then a law, that, when I would do good, evil is present with me (Rom. 7:21). It was Job, the perfect and upright man," who said, "I abhor myself." It was Daniel, eminently a man of God, who said, "My comeliness was turned in me into corruption," when he saw the glorified ancient of days.

Between these two natures there is conflict. Study carefully the battle between the two "I's": the old Saul and the new Paul in Romans 7:14-25. It is an experience like this which so discourages and perplexes young converts. The first joy of conversion has subsided, his glowing expectations become chilled, and the convert is dismayed to find the flesh with its old habits and desires within himself as before his conversion, and he is led to doubt his acceptance with God. This is a time of discouragement and danger. Paul in this crisis, cries out for deliverance, calling his old nature a "body of death." The law only intensifies his agony (though a converted man), and he finds deliverance from "the flesh," no through effort, nor through striving to keep the law, but "through Jesus Christ our Lord" (Rom. 7:24-25).

The presence of the flesh is not, however, an excuse for walking in it. We are taught that "our old man is crucified with Christ"; that, in that sense, we "are dead," and we are called upon to make this a constant experience by mortifying ("making dead") our members which are upon the earth.

The power for this is that of the Holy Spirit who dwells in every believer (I Cor. 6:19) and whose blessed office is to subdue the flesh. "This I say then, Walk in the Spirit, and ye shall not fulfil the lust of the flesh. For the flesh lusteth against the Spirit, and the Spirit against the flesh: and these are contrary the one to the other: so that ye cannot do the things that ye would." (Gal. 5:16-17).

"For if ye live after the flesh, ye shall die: but if ye through the Spirit do mortify the deeds of the body, ye shall live" (Rom. 8:13). Therefore, instead of meeting the solicitations of the old nature by force of will, or by good resolutions, turn the conflict over to the indwelling Spirit of God.

Romans 7 is a record of the conflict of regenerate man with his old self, and is, therefore, intensely personal. "I would," "I do not," "I would not," "I do," is the sad confession of defeat which finds an echo in so many Christian hearts. In chapter 8 the conflict still goes on, but how blessedly impersonal! There is no agony, for Paul is out of it; the conflict is now between "flesh"Saul of Tarsus-and the Holy Spirit. Paul is at peace and victorious. (It will be understood that this refers to victory over the flesh, such inward solicitations to evil as lust, pride, anger, etc.; temptations from without are met by recourse to Christ our high priest).

Consider attentively the following passages: "Knowing this, that our old man is crucified with him, that the body of sin might be destroyed [annulled, rendered powerless] that henceforth we should not serve sin" (Rom. 6:6).

"For we are the circumcision, which worship God in the Spirit, and rejoice in Christ Jesus, and have no confidence in the flesh" (Phil. 3:3).

"For ye are dead [have died-in Christ], and your life is hid with Christ in God" (Col. 3:3).

"Likewise reckon ye also yourselves to be dead indeed unto sin, but alive unto God through Jesus Christ our Lord" (Rom. 6: 11).

"But put ye on the Lord Jesus Christ, and make not provision for the flesh to fulfil the lusts thereof' (Rom. 13:14).

"Therefore, brethren, we are debtors, not to the flesh, to live after the flesh" (Rom. 8:12).

Chapter 8
THE BELIEVER'S STANDING AND STATE

A distinction of vast importance to the right understanding of the Scriptures, especially of the Epistles, is that which concerns the standing or position of the believer, and his state, or walk. The first is the result of the work of Christ and is perfect and entire from the very moment that Christ is received by faith. Nothing in the afterlife of the believer adds in the smallest degree to his title of favor with God, nor to his perfect security. Through faith alone this standing before God is conferred, and before Him the weakest person, if he be but a true believer on the Lord Jesus Christ, has precisely the same title as the most illustrious saint.

What that title or standing is, may be briefly seen from the following Scriptures: "But as many as received him, to them gave he power to become the sons of God, even to them that believe on his name" (John 1:12).

"Whosoever believeth that Jesus is the Christ is born of God" (I John 5:1).

"And if children, then heirs; heirs of God, and joint heirs with Christ" (Rom. 8:17).

"To an inheritance incorruptible, and undefiled, and that fadeth not away, reserved in heaven for you, who are kept by the power of God through faith unto salvation ready to be revealed in the last time" 0 Pet. 1:4-5).

"In whom also we have obtained an inheritance" (Eph. 1: 11).

"Beloved, now are we the sons of God; and it doth not ye appear what we shall be: but we know that, when he shall appear,
we shall be like him" (I John 3:2).

"But ye are a chosen generation, a royal priesthood, an holy nation" (I Pet. 2:9).

"Unto him that loved us, and washed us from our sins in his own blood, and hath made us kings and priests unto God and his Father" (Rev. 1:5-6).

"And ye are complete in him, which is the head of all principality and power" (Col. 2: 10).

"Therefore being justified by faith, we have peace with God through our Lord Jesus Christ: by whom also we have access by faith into this grace wherein we stand, and rejoice in hope of the glory of God" (Rom. 5:1-2).

"For God so loved the world, that he gave his only begotten Son, that whosoever believeth in him should not perish, but have everlasting life" (John 3:16).

"These things have I written unto you that believe on the name of the Son of God; that ye may know that ye have eternal life" (I John 5:13).

"Having therefore, brethren, boldness to enter into the holiest by the blood of Jesus" (Heb. 10: 19).

"Blessed be the God and Father of our Lord Jesus Christ, who hath blessed us with all- spiritual blessings" (Eph. 1:3).

"To the praise of the glory of his grace, wherein he hath made us accepted in the beloved" (Eph. 1:6).

"But God, who is rich in mercy, for his great love wherewith he loved us, even when we were dead in sins, hath quickened us together with Christ (by grace ye are saved), and hath raised us up together, and made us sit together in heavenly places in Christ Jesus" (Eph. 2:4-6).

"But now, in Christ Jesus, ye who sometime were far off, are made nigh by the blood of Chfist" (Eph. 2:13).

"In whom also, after that ye believed, ye were sealed with that Holy Spirit of promise" (Eph. 1: 13).

"For by one Spirit are we all baptized into one body" (I Cor. 12:13).

"For we are members of his body, of his flesh, and of his bones" (Eph. 5:30).

"What? know ye not that your body is the temple of the Holy Ghost?" (I Cor. 6:19).

Every one of these marvelous things is true of every believer on the Lord Jesus Christ. Not one item in this glorious inventory is said to be gained by prayer, or diligence in service, or churchgoing, or alms- giving, or self-denial, or holiness of life, or by any other description of good works. All are gifts of God through Christ and therefore belong equally to all believers. When the jailor of Philippi believed on the Lord Jesus Christ he became at once a child of God, a joint heir with Christ, a king and priest, and had the title to the incorruptible, undefiled, and unfading inheritance. In the instant that he believed with his heart and confessed with his mouth that Jesus was his Lord, he was justified from all things, had peace with God, a standing in His grace, and a sure hope of glory. He received the gift of eternal life, was made accepted in the full measure of Christ's own acceptance, was indwelt by, and sealed with the Holy Spirit, by whom also he was baptized into the mystical body of Christ- the church of God. Instantly he was clothed with the righteousness of God (Rom. 3:22), quickened with Christ, raised with Him, and in Him seated in the heavenlies.

What his actual state may have been is quite another mattercertainly it was far, far below his exalted standing in the sight of God. It was not all at once that he became as royal, priestly, and heavenly in walk as he was at once in standing. The following passages will indicate the way one's standing and one's state are constantly discriminated in the Scriptures.
STANDING
"Unto the church of God which is at Corinth, to them that are sanctified in Christ Jesus . . . I thank my God always on your behalf, for the grace of God which is given you by Jesus Christ that in every thing ye are enriched by him, in all utterance, and in all knowledge; even as the testimony of Christ was confirmed in you: so that ye come behind in no gift; waiting for the coming of our Lord Jesus Christ: who shall also confirm you unto the end, that ye may be blameless in the day of our Lord Jesus Christ. God is faithful, by whom ye were called unto the fellowship of his Son Jesus Christ" (I Cor. 1:2-9).

"But ye are washed, but ye are sanctified, but ye are justified in the name of the Lord Jesus, and by the Spirit of our God" (I Cor. 6:11).

"Know ye not that your bodies are the members of Christ?" (I Cor. 6:15).

"And Jesus answered and said unto him, Blessed art thou, Simon Bar-jona: for flesh and blood hath not revealed it unto thee, but my Father which is in heaven" (Matt. 16:17).

"Giving thanks unto the Father, which hath made us meet to be partakers of the inheritance of the saints in light: who hath delivered us from the power of darkness, and hath translated us into the kingdom of his dear Son" (Col. 1: 12-13).

STATE

"For it hath been declared unto me of you, my brethren, by them which are of the house of Chloe, that there are contentions among you" (I Cor. 1:11).

"And 1, brethren, could not speak unto you as unto spiritual, but as unto carnal . . . For ye are yet carnal: for whereas there is among you envying, and strife, and divisions, are ye not carnal, and walk as men?" (I Cor. 3:1-3).

"Now some are puffed up" (I Cor. 4:18).

"And ye are puffed up, and have not rather mourned, that he that hath done this deed might be taken away from among you" (I Cor. 5:2).

"Now therefore there is utterly a fault among you, because ye go to law one with another" (I Cor. 6:7).

"Shall I then take the members of Christ, and make them the members of an harlot?" (I Cor. 6:15).

"But he turned, and said unto Peter, Get thee behind me, Satan; for thou art an offence unto me; for thou savorest not the things that be of God, but those that be of men" (Matt. 16:23).

"But now ye also put off all these; anger, wrath, malice, blasphemy, filthy communication out of your mouth. Lie not one to another, seeing that ye have put off the old man with his deeds" (Col. 3:8-9).

The student cannot fail to notice that the divine order, under grace, is first to give the highest possible standing and then to exhort the believer to maintain a state in accordance therewith. The beggar is lifted up from the dung-hill and set among princes (I Sam. 2:8), and then exhorted to be princely. As examples, see the following verses.

STANDING

"Knowing this, that our old man is crucified with him, that the body of sin might be destroyed" (Rom. 6:6).

"Ye are the light of the world" (Matt. 5:14).

"Who hath saved us, and called us with an holy calling, not according to our works, but according to his own purpose and grace, which was given us in Christ Jesus before the world began" (2 Tim. 1:9).

"And hath raised us up together, and made us sit together in heavenly places in Christ Jesus" (Eph. 2:6).

"When Christ, who is our life, shall appear, then shall ye also appear with him in glory" (Col. 3:4).

"For ye were sometimes darkness, but now are ye light in the Lord" (Eph. 5:8).

"Ye are all the children of light, and the children of the day: we are not of the night, nor of darkness" (I Thess. 5:5).

"For God hath not appointed us to wrath, but to obtain salvation by our Lord Jesus Christ, who died for us, that, whether we wake or sleep, we should live together with him" (I Thess. 5:9-10).

"By the which will we are sanctified, through the offering of the body of Jesus Christ once for all" (Heb. 10:10).
"But of him are ye in Christ Jesus, who of God is made unto us . . . sanctification" (I Cor. 1:30).

"For by one offering he hath perfected forever them that are sanctified" (Heb. 10:14).

"Let us therefore, as many as be perfect, be thus minded" (Phil. 3:15).

"Herein is our love made perfect, that we may have boldness in the day of judgment: because as he is, so are we in this world" (I John 4:17).
STATE
"Wherefore if ye be dead with Christ from the rudiments of the world, why, as though living in the world, are ye subject to ordinances?" (Col. 2:20).

"Let your light so shine before men, that they may see your good works, and glorify your Father which is in heaven" (Matt. 5:16).

"Wherefore, my beloved, as ye have always obeyed, not as in my presence only, but now much more in my absence, work out your own salvation with fear and trembling" (Phil. 2:12). (Let it be observed, in reading this much-abused text, that the salvation spoken of here is not that of the soul, but salvation out of the snares which would hinder the Christian from doing the will of God.)

"If ye then be risen with Christ, seek those things which are above, where Christ sitteth on the right hand of God" (Col. 3: 1).

"Mortify therefore your members which are upon the earth" (Col. 3:5).

"Walk as children of light" (Eph. 5:8).

"Therefore let us not sleep, as do others; but let us watch and be sober" (I Thess. 5:6).

"Wherefore comfort yourselves together, and edify one another, even as also ye do" (I Thess. 5:11).

"Sanctify them through thy truth: thy word is truth" (John 17:17).

"And the very God of peace sanctify you wholly" (I Thess. 5:23).

"Not as though I had already attained, either were already perfect" (Phil. 3:12).

"Therefore, leaving the principles of the doctrine of Christ, let us go on unto perfection" (Heb. 6: 1).

"He that saith he abideth in him, ought himself also so to walk, even as he walked" (I John 2:6).

The student will be able to add largely to this list of comparative passages showing that the Scripture makes a clear distinction between the standing and state of the believer. It will be seen that he is not under probation to see if he is worthy of an inconceivably exalted position, but, beginning with the confession of his utter unworthiness, receives the position wholly as the result of Christ's work. Positionally he is "perfected forever" (Heb. 10: 14), but looking within, at his state, he must say, "Not as though I had already attained, either were already perfect" (Phil. 3:12).

It may be said that all the afterwork of God in his behalf, the application of the Word to his walk and conscience (John 17:17; Eph. 5:26), the chastisements of the Father's hand (Heb. 12:10; 1 Cor. 11:32), the ministry of the Spirit (Eph. 4:11-12), all the difficulties and trials of the wilderness way (I Pet. 4:12-14), and the final transformation when He shall appear (I John 3:2), all are intended simply to bring the believer's character into perfect conformity to the position which is his in the instant of his conversion. He grows in grace, indeed, but not into grace.

A prince, while he is a little child, is presumably as willful and as ignorant as other little children. Sometimes he may be very obedient and teachable and affectionate, and then he is happy and approved; at other times he may be unruly, self-willed, and disobedient, and then he is unhappy and perhaps is chastised. But he is just as much a prince on the one day as on the other. It may be hoped that, as time goes on, he will learn to bring himself into willing and affectionate subjection to every right way, and then he will be more princely, but not more really a prince. He was born a prince.

In the case of every true son of the King of kings, and Lord of lords, this growth into kingliness is assured. In the end, standing and state, character and position, will be equal. But the position is not the reward of the perfected character-the character is developed from the position.

Chapter 9
SALVATION AND REWARDS

The New Testament Scriptures contain a doctrine of salvation for sinners who are lost and a doctrine of rewards for the faithful services of those who are saved. And it is of great importance to the right understanding of the Word that the student should clearly make the distinction between these. What that distinction is may be seen by carefully noting the following contrasts.

SALVATION IS A FREE GIFT

"Jesus answered and said unto her, If thou knewest the gift of God, and who it is that saith to thee, Give me to drink; thou wouldest have asked of him, and he would have given thee living water" (John 4:10).

"Ho, every one that thirsteth, come ye to the waters, and he that hath no money; come ye, buy, and eat; yea, come, buy wine and milk without money and without price" (Isa. 55:1).

"And the Spirit and the bride say, Come. And let him that heareth say, Come. And let him that is athirst come: and whosoever will, let him take the water of life freely" (Rev. 22:17).

"For the wages of sin is death; but the gift of God is eternal life, through Jesus Christ our Lord" (Rom. 6:23).

"For by grace are ye saved through faith; and that not of yourselves: it is the gift of God: not of works lest any man should boast" (Eph. 2:8-9).

But in contrast with the freeness of salvation, note that those works that are pleasing to God shall be rewarded.

WORKS PLEASING TO GOD SHALL BE REWARDED

"And whosoever shall give to drink unto one of these little ones a cup of cold water only in the name of a disciple, verily I say unto you, he shall in no wise lose his reward" (Matt. 10:42).

"I have fought a good fight, I have finished my course, I have kept the faith: henceforth there is laid up for me a crown of righteousness" (2 Tim. 4:7-8).

"And, behold, I come quickly; and my reward is with me, to give every man according as his work shall be" (Rev. 22:12).

"Know ye not that they which run in a race run all, but one receiveth the prize? So run, that ye may obtain. And every man that striveth for the mastery is temperate in all things. Now they do it to obtain a corruptible crown; but we an incorruptible" (I Cor 9:24-25).

'And he said unto him, Well, thou good servant: because thou hast been faithful in a very little, have thou authority over ten cities" (Luke 19:17).

"For other foundation can no man lay than that is laid, which Is Jesus Christ. Now if any man build upon this foundation gold, silver, precious stones, wood, hay, stubble; every man's work shall he made manifest: for the day shall declare it, because it shall be revealed by fire; and the fire shall try every man's work of what sort it is. If any man's work abide which he hath built thereupon, he shall receive a reward. If any man's work shall be burned, he shall suffer loss: but he himself shall be saved; yet so as by fire" (I Cor. 3:11-15).

"Fear none of those things which thou shalt suffer: behold, the devil shall cast some of you into prison, that ye may be tried; and ye shall have tribulation ten days: be thou faithful unto death, and I will give thee a crown of life" (Rev. 2: 10). Not receive life-the suffering saints in Smyrna had life, eternal life, and were suffering for righteousness' sake-but a crown of life they should receive.

Crowns are symbols of rewards, of distinctions earned. It may be remarked that four crowns are mentioned: that of joy, or rejoicing, the reward of ministry (Phil. 4:1; 1 Thess. 2:19); of righteousness, the reward of faithfulness in testimony (2 Tim. 4:8); of life, the reward of faithfulness under trial (James 1: 12; Rev. 2: 10); of glory, the reward of faithfulness under suffering (I Pet. 5:4; Heb. 2:9).

SALVATION IS A PRESENT POSSESSION

"He that believeth on the Son hath everlasting life" (John 3:36).

"Verily, verily, I say unto you, He that heareth my word, and believeth on him that sent me, hath everlasting life, and shall not come into condemnation; but is passed from death unto life." (John 5:24).

"Verily, verily, I say unto you, He that believeth on me hath everlasting life" (John 6:47).

"Who hath saved us, and called us with a holy calling, not according to our works, but according to his own purpose and grace" (2 Tim. 1:9).

"And he said to the woman, Thy faith hath saved thee; go in peace" (Luke 7:50).

"Not by works of righteousness which we have done, but according to his mercy he saved us, by the washing of regeneration, and renewing of the Holy Ghost" (Titus 3:5).

"And this is the record, that God hath given to us eternal life, and this life is in his Son" (I John 5: 11).

But these rewards are to be given at a future time.
REWARDS ARE BESTOWED IN THE FUTURE
"For the Son of man shall come in the glory of his Father, with his angels; and then he shall reward every man according to his works" (Matt. 16:27).

"For thou shalt be recompensed at the resurrection of the just" (Luke 14:14).

"And, behold, I come quickly; and my reward is with me, to give every man according as his work shall be" (Rev. 22:12).

"And when the chief Shepherd shall appear, ye shall receive a crown of glory that fadeth not away" (I Pet. 5:4).

"Henceforth there is laid up for me a crown of righteousness, which the Lord, the righteous judge, shall give me at that day" (2 Tim. 4:8).

"After a long time the lord of those servants cometh, and reckoneth with them" (Matt. 25:19).

God's purpose in promising to reward with heavenly and eternal honors the faithful service of His saints is to win them from the pursuit of earthly riches and pleasures, to sustain them in the fires of persecution, and to encourage them in the exercise of Christian virtues. "Finally, let us heed the warning" (Rev. 3: 11). (See Dan. 12:3; Matt. 5:11-12; Matt. 10:41-42; Luke 12:35-37; Luke 14:12, 14; John 4:35-36; Col. 3:22-24; 2 Tim. 4:8; Heb. 6: 10; Heb. 11:8-10, 24-27; Heb. 12:2- 3.)

Chapter 10
BELIEVERS AND PROFESSORS

Ever since God has had a people separated to Himself they have been sorely troubled by the presence among them of those who professed to be, but were not, of them. And this will continue until "the Son of man shall send forth his angels, and they shall Sober out of his kingdom all things that offend, and them which do inquity... Then shall the righteous shine forth as the sun in the kingdom of their Father" (Matt. 13:14-43).

Scripture plainly tells us of this mingling of tares and wheat-of mere professors among true believers. Yet misguided students have frequently applied to the children of God the warnings and exhortations meant only for the self-deceived or hypocritical.

The fact of such admixture is abundantly recognized in the Scriptures. (See Gen. 4:3-5; Exod. 12:38; Num. 11:4-6; Neh. 7:63-65; Neh. 13:1-3; Matt. 13:24-30, 37-43; 2 Cor. 11: 13-15; Gal. 2:4; 2 Pet. 2:1-2.

It is impossible, in a brief Bible reading, to refer to all the passages which discriminate true believers from the mass of mere formalists, hypocrites, or deceived legalists, who are working for their own salvation instead of working out a salvation already received as a free gift. (See Phil. 2:12-13 with Eph. 2:8-9.) The following comparison of verses will sufficiently indicate the lines of demarcation.

BELIEVERS ARE SAVED; MERE PROFESSORS ARE LOST
TRUE BELIEVERS

"And he said to the woman, Thy faith hath saved thee; go in peace" (Luke 7:50).

"And they continued stedfastly in the apostles' doctrine and fellowship, and in breaking of bread, and in prayers" (Acts 2:42).

"My sheep hear my voice, and I know them, and they follow me: and I give unto them eternal life; and they shall never perish, neither shall any man pluck them out of my hand. My Father, which gave them me, is greater than all; and no man is able to pluck them out of my Father's hand" (John 10:27-29).

"All that the Father giveth me shall come to me; and him that cometh to me I will in no wise cast out. And this is the Father's will which hath sent me, that of all which he hath given me I should lose nothing, but should raise it up again at the last day" (John 6:37,39).

"And while they went to buy, the bridegroom came; and they that were ready went in with him to the marriage: and the door was shut" (Matt. 25:10).

"Even the righteousness of God which is by faith of Jesus Christ, unto all and upon all them that believe: for there is no difference" (Rom. 3:22).

"Let us be glad and rejoice, and give honour to him: for the marriage of the Lamb is come, and his wife hath made herself ready. And to her was granted that she should be arrayed in fine linen, clean and white: for the fine linen is the righteousness of saints." (Rev 19:7-8).

I am the good shepherd, and know my sheep, and am known of mine" (John 10: 14).

"Nevertheless the foundation of God standeth sure, having this seal, The Lord knoweth them that are his" (2 Tim. 2:19).

"Verily, verily, I say unto you, He that believeth on me hath everlasting life" (John 6:47).

"Father, I will that they also, whom thou hast given me, be with me where I am; that they may behold my glory, which thou hast given me: for thou lovedst me before the foundation of the world" (John 17:24).

"Being confident of this very thing, that he which hath begun a good work in you, will perform it until the day of Jesus Christ" (Phil. 1:6).

"But we are not of them who draw back unto perdition, but of them that believe to the saving of the soul" (Heb. 10:39).

PRETENDERS

"Then Simon himself believed also: and when he was baptized, be continued with Philip. But Peter said unto him ... Thou hast neither part nor lot in this matter: for thy heart is not right in the *ht of God" (Acts 8:13,21).

"They went out from us, but they were not of us; for if they bad been of us, they would no doubt have continued with us: but they went out, that they might be made manifest that they were not all of us" (John 2:19).

"But there are some of you that believe not. For Jesus knew from the beginning who they were that believed not, and who should betray him. And he said, Therefore said I unto you, that no man can come unto me, except it were given unto him of my Father. From that time many of his disciples went back, and walked no more with him" (John 6:64-66).

"Afterward came also the other virgins, saying, Lord, Lord, open to us. But he answered and said, Verily I say unto you, I know you not" (Matt. 25:11-12).

"Even so ye also outwardly appear righteous unto men, but within ye are full of hypocrisy and iniquity. Ye serpents, ye generation of vipers! how can ye escape the damnation of hell?" (Matt. 23:28,33).
"And when the king came in to see the guests, he saw there a man which had not on a wedding garment: and he saith unto him, Friend, how camest thou in hither not having a wedding garment? And he was speechless. Then said the king to the servants, Bind him hand and foot, and take him away, and cast him into outer darkness" (Matt. 22:11-13).

"Many will say to me in that day, Lord, Lord, have we not prophesied in thy name? and in thy name have cast out devils? and in thy name done many wonderful works? And then will I profess unto them, I never knew you: depart from me, ye that work iniquity" (Matt. 7:22-23).

"What doth it profit, my brethren, though a man say he hath faith, and have not works? can faith save him?" (James 2:14).

"For it is impossible for those who were once enlightened, and have tasted of the heavenly gift, and were made partakers of the Holy Ghost, and have tasted the good word of God, and the powers of the world to come, if they shall fall away, to renew them again unto repentance" (Heb. 6:4-6).

"Now the just shall live by faith: but if any man draw back, my soul shall have no pleasure in him" (Heb. 10:38).
BELIEVERS ARE REWARDED; PRETENDERS ARE CONDEMNED
Compare: Matthew 25:19-23 with Matthew 25:24-30; Luke 12:42-44 with Luke 12:45-47; Colossians 3:24 with Matthew 7:22-23.

Some texts are not free from difficulty, but with prayer and careful study light will surely come when keeping in mind the important rule: Never use a doubtful or obscure passage to contradict a clear and positive one. Do not use an "if" to contradict a "verily": Hebrews 6:6 to contradict John 5:24.

The cases of Judas Iscariot and of Peter should present no difficulty. Judas was never a believer; (see John 6:68-71). Peter never ceased to be one (Luke 22:31-32).

It should be ever remembered that these principles are to guide us only in rightly dividing the Word of God, but are never to be applied to living persons. The judgment of professors is not committed to us, but is reserved to the Son of Man (Matt. 13:28-29; 1 Cor. 4:5).

Abbreviated Bibliography

Rightly Dividing the Word of Truth
Written by C.I Scofield
Public Domain

All Quotes referencing John MacArthur
© 2016 Grace to You. All rights reserved.
PO Box 4000
Panorama City, California 91412

Quotes related to Theopedia
The 'textual' content of Theopedia, unless otherwise noted, is under the Creative Commons Attribution 3.0 Unported license. This means it may be copied, distributed, transmitted, and adapted, provided that attribution is given to Theopedia.com and the license terms are made clear.
When using content from an article, take note of any images that are not under our Creative Commons license. Images are often used in accordance with fair use.

References marked Got Questions are
© Copyright 2002-2016 Got Questions Ministries -
All Rights Reserved. 1

Made in the USA
Las Vegas, NV
06 March 2021